CLASSIC AND SPORTSCAR

JAGUAR E-TYPE FILE

CLASSIC AND SPORTSCAR

JAGUAR E-TYPE FILE

3.8 • 4.2 • V12

MARTIN
BUCKLEY

Series Editor Mark Hughes

TEMPLE PRESS

First published 1988 by
Temple Press
an imprint of
The Hamlyn Publishing Group Ltd
a division of
The Octopus Group PLC
Michelin House, 81 Fulham Road
London SW3 6RB
and distributed for them by
Octopus Distribution Services Ltd
Rushden, Northants NN10 9RZ

Produced by Bay View Books Ltd
Bideford, Devon EX39 2QE
Designed by Gerrard Lindley
Special photography by John Colley
Picture research by Jon Pressnell
Typeset by Lens Typesetting, Bideford
Reproduction by Isca Reprographics, Exeter

ISBN 0 0600 55781 2
Printed in Hong Kong

Contents

A Classic Combination 6

Performance Figures 18

E-Type 3.8 and 4.2 19

E-Type 5.3 V12 79

Production History 95

Production Figures 105

Clubs 106

Specialists 108

Acknowledgments 110

A Classic Combination

No other British sports car has ever caught the motoring public's imagination in quite the same way as the Jaguar E-type. Its combination of fabulous looks, exhilarating performance and an almost unbelievably low price caused a sensation back in 1961, and for the best part of 14 years afterwards Jaguar's sporting flagship was *the* car to be seen in. Even now, well over 25 years after its introduction, the E-type is still the pinnacle of many drivers' ambitions.

3.8-litre

The E-type was produced in four basic forms between 1961 and 1975, and according to some experts it's the original 3.8-litre car, built up to 1964, that has the most charisma, in spite of its many annoying flaws. In terms of styling it was a gorgeous-looking machine in either closed or open forms, a swoopy, elegant D-type inspired shape with hunched hindquarters, a long snouted bonnet, faired-in headlights, and that delicate oval air intake. The best possible aerodynamics may have been at the forefront of Malcolm Sayer's mind when he penned the E-type, but more importantly he created perhaps the most beautiful and instantly recognizable shape of the sixties into the bargain.

Under the bonnet lurked a 3781cc version of the immortal XK in-line six, generally thought to be the finest version of this classic double overhead camshaft design. Producing 265bhp with its three 2in SU carbs and 'straight port' cylinder head, it was a smooth but wonderfully lusty sounding unit that provided the E with brilliant straight line performance and uncanny low speed flexibility. OK, so few owners ever saw the famed 150mph top speed achieved with 'improved' road test cars of the day, but a true 143mph was certainly available and, more to the point, 125mph was a mere gallop.

Acceleration varied according to the axle ratio, but generally 60mph could be achieved

below

The inspiration for the E-type came directly from D-type sports racing car first seen in 1954. A Le Mans winner in 1955, '56 and '57, like the E it had a monocoque centre section, a front subframe supporting the XK engine and double wishbone and torsion bar front suspension, though a beam axle was used at the back. The efficient shape of the car was by Malcolm Sayer and is obviously very closely related to his E-type design.

right

The XKSS was another small step towards the production E-type, being a road going version of the D-type.

below

This car, E2A, was an experimental sports racing machine built after Jaguar had stopped racing in the late fifties, and quite apart from looking very like the E-type shared many of its engineering features: a central stressed monocoque, a non-stressed bonnet and a detachable subframe, but the really big news was the independent rear suspension, which featured all the essential aspects of the E-type unit except for the trailing radius arms and the famous steel subframe 'cradle'. The car made an ill-fated appearance at Le Mans in 1960 and was rarely seen afterwards.

top

This model made by Malcolm Sayer in 1954 shows all the basic E-type styling elements.

left and below

The first full-size prototype, photographed on the Browns Lane playing fields. Note the absence of bonnet louvres and of the bar across the air intake, among other details.

The E-type in its natural element – hood down on traffic free roads. This is a 3.8-litre car.

The shape was just as sensational from the rear. The hood was reasonably watertight and rearward visibility not as bad as some.

Malcolm Sayer's unmistakable outline, perhaps the best known shape in post-war sports car history. This 1961 roadster is a concours car owned by Mark Hamilton of Hampson Motor Trust.

A classic workmanlike cockpit with the big handsome wood-rimmed wheel, large white-on-black Smiths instruments and a typically confusing line-up of toggle switches. Only 3.8-litre cars had the aluminium finish on instrument panel and centre console.

The classic 265bhp 3.8-litre XK engine, with three 2in SU carbs and the 'straight port' cylinder head. A virtually identical unit was used in the 3.8 XK150S and the 3.8 Mk X saloon. It used plenty of oil in its early years and – in the E – always ran hot, but many will tell you it is the best XK engine of them all.

top

The 3.8 E-type roadster as it appeared in March 1961. All Series 1 cars had glass headlight covers and wire wheels where standard. The external bonnet lock identifies this as a very early car.

above

The E-type fixed-head coupé, announced alongside the roadster. 7669 3.8 fixed-head coupés were built up to 1964.

in a very vivid 7 seconds (second gear ran to 74mph with the 3.31:1 final drive) and 100mph in a shade over 18 seconds. Road test 3.8s rarely delivered standing quarter mile times of much over 15 seconds, which is very quick indeed.

In spite of all this performance the E-type was no highly strung racer, its 206lb ft of torque making it superbly tractable in top gear, so much so that it was quite possible to run down to a walking pace in top and accelerate smoothly and swiftly away. It wasn't a thirsty car either, 18mpg being a typical overall consumption figure.

Keeping the E-type's brawn in check was a stiff monocoque chassis, with independent suspension at both ends – torsion bars and wishbones at the front and at the rear a combination of upper and lower wishbones/ drive shafts with coil springs and radius arms. This set-up gave excellent, basically neutral handling characteristics, the best technique being to keep the power on round corners, which made the steering lighter and merely increased the drift angle as the car accelerated, the Dunlop tyres allowing excellent wet or dry road adhesion by the standards of the day. At a very high limit the back end would eventually break away, but very controllably, and of course the accelerator needed to be treated with greater respect in wet weather with so much torque on hand. Front and rear anti-roll bars kept the roll angles low. The E-type was also blessed with high-geared rack and pinion steering which was nicely weighted (but not too heavy) and gave plenty of feel and even a bit of kick-back on bumpy roads. This high gearing and lack of run-wide understeer made the E a responsive and agile machine, and it's probably safe to say that nothing short of a Lotus Elite could catch a well-driven example on a twisty road.

Another remarkable feature of the E-type was its ride, which for a sports car was soft, comfortable and the equal of many saloon cars of the day. Gone was the harsh, vertical bouncing of the old breed of high-performance machines – the E simply smothered severe bumps at speed and if not exactly 'boulevard' around town it was much better than any other sports car. The E-type was also a mechanically quiet car and in closed form there was little wind noise.

But astonishing as it was in so many respects, the 3.8 E-type did have a number of faults, chief among these being the Moss four-speed gearbox which Jaguar owners had been

3.8s on the production line at Browns Lane.

The E-type's racing debut in the GT Class at Oulton Park in April 1961. The Equipe Endeavour roadster (ECD 400) came in first, driven by Graham Hill, beating Ferrari and Aston Martin. The Coombs-prepared car BUY 1 was driven by Roy Salvadori and came in a creditable third. In spite of this encouraging start the E-type's racing career was always steady rather than spectacular.

suffering since well before the days of the XK120. Bottom gear had no synchromesh at all and the lever would frequently baulk going into the other forward ratios. The four-wheel Dunlop disc brakes, with the bellows servo, were also slightly dubious, being rather susceptible to delayed pedal action and even fade in very extreme use. The XK engine was not beyond criticism either on early cars, using oil at the rate of 200 to 300 miles per pint and having a somewhat marginal cooling system that boiled up easily and only served to emphasize the very poor cockpit ventilation and gearbox tunnel insulation.

Another big problem was accommodation. Quite simply, anyone six feet tall or over had great difficulty in shoehorning himself into the E-type, and once installed usually found that his knees were fouling the steering wheel due to the lack of rearward seat adjustment, the fixed backrest and the totally flat floor. Headroom was also limited, and although the bucket seats looked good most people found them pretty uncomfortable, causing backache and providing little side support or padding. The hood worked well at least, and although the roadster had little usable boot space the fixed-head coupé had quite a generous load area easily accessible through the side-hinged rear door.

4.2-litre

Jaguar answered criticisms of the original 3.8 E-type with the 4.2 of 1964, which in almost every way was a far better and more practical everyday car. It looked just as good as the 3.8, went just as well (better, according to some tests, despite the increase in weight) and above all it was still outstanding value for money; when first introduced the 4.2 coupé cost £1992, compared with £3323 for a Corvette Stingray which didn't handle as well and £2277 for a much slower Porsche 1600SC.

Though the 4.2 engine perhaps wasn't *quite* as sweet as the smaller unit, it had even greater usable torque and nothing like the same appetite for oil, although to be fair the later 3.8 engines were much improved in this respect. The best news of all, however, was the fitment of a brand new Jaguar designed and built four-speed all-synchromesh gearbox giving a far smoother, lighter and quicker change that was actually a pleasure to use. The brakes were better too, the more conventional Lockheed servo allowing better feel and progression.

Proper front footwells and more seat adjustment had been added to the 3.8 during its production run but the new car went a useful step further with bigger, more comfortable seats with adjustable squabs. The sum total of these changes was a much more habitable E-type – perhaps the version to go for today if you want a car you can regularly use in some degree of comfort. First-of-the-breed appeal of the rough and ready 3.8 apart, the first series 4.2 cars are arguably the best E-types of the lot.

For the family man there was a 2-plus-2 E-type from 1966 onwards, the extra length and higher roofline spoiling the shape a little but giving room for a reasonably useful rear seat that could accommodate two small children on long journeys or a couple of adults on shorter trips. Luggage accommodation was better with the rear seats folded, too.

The performance was down to a still good 140mph (the 2-plus-2 was nearly 2cwt heavier) but lower gearbox ratios helped acceleration and flexibility. Ride comfort was thought to be a little better and handling was hardly affected apart perhaps from extra front end plunge and rather more sudden rear end break-away. On the 2-plus-2 body there was now room for an optional automatic gearbox, the Borg-Warner Model 8, cutting the performance down still further (136mph, 0-60 in 9.2 seconds) and giving none too smooth changes by the latest North American standards. Some said that the auto 'box also affected the handling adversely, as the lack of drive line rigidity made it impossible to alter the car's attitude in corners the way you could with the manual version.

The 2-plus-2 E-type is certainly the least popular of the six cylinder E-types (though the Americans always loved it) but this compromise model does at least have better accommodation and considerably lower market values on its side, so it's an attractive proposition for the enthusiast who desperately wants an E-type but can't afford a roadster or normal wheelbase coupé. Automatic cars are especially good value.

As far as serious drivers were concerned the rot started to set in when the Series 2 models came along late in 1968. Weight was up, performance was slightly down, and appearance suffered thanks to open headlights (though these had actually been seen first on the so called 'Series 1½' the year before), a bigger air intake, and much less subtle squared-up tail lights mounted below the bumper. Most of these changes were in response to ever tightening safety and emission regulations and American E-type buyers faced even more changes, cars destined for their market being fitted with a

With the introduction of the Series 2 in 1968 the E started to put on middle-aged spread and lose some of its good looks, not to mention a little performance. The glass headlight covers had actually disappeared in 1967 on the so-called Series 1½, though the Series 2 had thicker headlight surrounds and a more obtrusive bar in the bigger air intake. The new indicators were mounted under the bumper.

low-powered, two-carburettor, de-toxed engine that cut the performance down rather dramatically; a Stateside Series 2 roadster would have had trouble seeing a true 130mph, which was a far cry from the original macho 3.8 of only seven years earlier. Having said that, a good European spec. Series 2 should not be too much slower off the mark than a Series 1 and does offer certain advantages, such as better cooling and improved comfort.

5.3-litre

The Series 3 V12 E-type provoked very mixed reactions when it was first seen in 1971. Without exception all conceded that the new all-alloy 60 degree V12 was an engineering masterpiece, and almost certainly the finest production engine in the world. With a true 272bhp net on hand (the XK's output was expressed in dubious gross terms) this new powerhouse endowed the heavier Series 3 with a top speed almost equal to that of a 'Press prepared' Series 1 3.8 or 4.2 (146mph), and the 5.3 also enjoyed even more impressive acceleration – manual roadsters recorded 0 to 60 times as low as 6.4 seconds and could attain 110mph in the same time it took a good six-cylinder car to reach 100mph.

The unit had real steam-train flexibility, its 304lb ft of torque at 3400rpm allowing a very beefy surge of top-gear thrust that could pull the car smoothly from under 500rpm. In terms of mid-range acceleration this meant that between 40 and 80mph every 10mph increment took just 2.8 seconds in top gear, and the car was quite capable of accelerating in fourth all the way up to 110mph in just over 36 seconds! The four-speed gearbox coped reasonably well with the V12 engine (it offered maxima in the indirects of 52, 78 and 108mph) and of course there was an automatic option, now the somewhat smoother Borg-Warner Model 12. But perhaps the best thing about the new engine was its uncanny refinement. It was far smoother than the venerable XK six up to its higher 6500rpm red line and virtually inaudible up to 5000rpm, after which it emitted a smooth purr changing to a more mechanical noise over 6000rpm. There was never any suggestion of induction roar, and the exhaust gave out a pleasant mechanical hum rather than the lusty note of the XK-engined cars.

Splendid as this all-new engine was, enthusiasts who had been expecting a brand new 'F-type' were largely disappointed by the

The Series 3 V12 E-type of 1971 was a very different animal from its predecessors, the incredibly refined 272bhp engine bringing performance back to Series 1 levels but showing up the rest of the ageing chassis. New styling touches like the bigger 'birdcage' grille, flared arches and 2-plus-2 wheelbase for both open and closed models were not to everyone's taste, but today the V12 roadster is the most sought after and valuable E-type of all.

Series 3, which was little more than a thorough re-hash of the now 10-year-old design. Both open and closed versions of the V12 had the 2-plus-2's wheelbase, with flared wheel arches housing wider wheels and tyres, and a yet bigger front air intake with a full 'birdcage' grille, all of which gave the V12 a broader, more muscular look. Some liked the new style, others were less enthusiastic, but nobody could claim that the Series 3 re-captured the lean, elegant look of the Series 1.

On the road the whole feel of the Series 3 was softer, more biased towards comfort and ease of control than any previous E-type. The biggest detraction for serious drivers was the now standard Adwest power steering, which was responsive but much too light to give a proper indication of loss of front wheel adhesion and which made the car harder to place when correcting oversteer. The V12 still had rail-like cornering ability, though, and in fact the roadholding on the fatter XJ6-size tyres was considerably improved, though obviously the massive torque could easily overcome the rear wheels on tighter corners. There was little trace of body roll and the brakes – now ventilated discs at the front – were for once well up to the car's performance.

On the comfort front the high-speed ride was still excellent but the ventilation, accommodation and (in roadster form) noise suppression were well behind the times. By no stretch of the imagination were they good enough to compete with the luxury GT cars of the day. In short, the V12 was a classic example of a superb engine looking for a modern chassis, and it was rather sad that such an admired design as the E-type had been allowed to soldier on long after its best days had gone. To be perfectly fair, the Series 3 was still excellent value for money, and right up to its death in 1975 there was nothing as quick available for the same kind of price.

Currently the V12 E, particularly in roadster form, is the most sought-after of the E-type range, and this may have something to do with the fact that they are the easiest to live with, the most comfortable and the fastest of the lot. Average fuel consumption usually works out at around 14mpg, so a Series 3 will not be a cheap car to run.

With pace, looks and sophistication to match almost any Italian exotic, but at a fraction of the cost, the Jaguar E-type was in a class of its own for most of its 14-year production run. Today, although prices seem to be going through the roof, the cars are still pretty good value for money considering the wide range of abilities they offer. The E-type is also one of the few supercars of its era that doesn't come as a major disappointment when driven; a really good example on the right road can still be an inspiration. From a practical viewpoint the E-type has more than its fair share of flaws, as this book will highlight, yet for many people it still comes closer to the ideal than any other sports car of the sixties. It was a classic from the beginning and it always will be one.

PERFORMANCE FIGURES

	E-TYPE 3.8 Roadster	E-TYPE 3.8 Coupé	E-TYPE 4.2 S1 Roadster	E-TYPE 4.2 S1 Coupé
Max speed	149mph	150mph	149mph	150mph
0-60mph	7.1secs	6.9secs	7.4secs	7.0secs
Standing ¼ mile	15.0secs	14.7secs	15.0secs	14.9secs
Fuel consumption	19.7mpg	17.9mpg	21.8mpg	18.5mpg

	E-TYPE 4.2 S1 2-plus-2	E-TYPE 4.2 S2 Roadster	E-TYPE 4.2 S2 Coupé	E-TYPE 4.2 S2 2-plus-2 auto
Max speed	139mph	142mph	143mph	136mph
0-60mph	7.4secs	7.2secs	7.2secs	8.9secs
Standing ¼ mile	15.4secs	14.9secs	14.9secs	16.4secs
Fuel consumption	18.8mpg	18.5mpg	18.9mpg	18.3mpg

	E-TYPE 4.2* S2 Roadster	E-TYPE 5.3 S3 Roadster	E-TYPE 5.3 S3 2-plus-2	E-TYPE 5.3* S3 Roadster auto
Max speed	126mph	146mph	142mph	135mph
0-60mph	7.2secs	6.4secs	6.8secs	7.1secs
Standing ¼ mile	15.5secs	14.2secs	14.6secs	15.1secs
Fuel consumption	17.2mpg	14.5mpg	15.2mpg	14.0mpg

* Federal specification

Notes on performance

Though the idea was rather nice the E-type was never truly capable of a genuine two-way maximum of 150mph. Those early *Autocar* and *Motor* road test cars (registered 77RW and 9600HP) had blueprinted engines, and *Motor* noted that 77RW pinked on 100 octane fuel at 2000-2500rpm and exhibited some fluffiness in traffic on the standard plugs . . . The maximum speed was achieved on special Dunlop R5 racing tyres, too. Furthermore the cars were lightened somewhat, 9600HP (a Geneva Show press demonstrator coupé) having an aluminium rear door and Perspex side windows. 'Improving' these early test cars in this way meant that Jaguar had to ensure that every subsequent test E-type was capable of at least 150mph! However, a standard Series 1 or European specification Series 2 would still beat 140mph in two-seater form, making the E one of the fastest cars in the world during the sixties. Series 3 cars went out in standard tune for road test, as far as I know. If anything, a good V12 should outrun a six-cylinder car in a straight line.

E-type 3.8 and 4.2

The E-type of 1961 was created as a direct replacement for the XK150 range, and in virutally every aspect of design and construction it was light years ahead of this last of the XK line. Where the E used an advanced unitary body with sleek aerodynamic lines and independent suspension at both ends, the 150 made do with a rough-and-ready separate chassis, cart sprung at the rear and topped by an attractive but fairly bluff body style that could trace its roots back to the original XK 120 of 1948. Quite simply, the E-type was a massive step forward, a sophisticated design for the much more demanding sixties that had little in common with its predecessor except the superb XK engine and that hard-to-define Jaguar look and feel.

Although they vary considerably in desirability and value all the six-cylinder E-types share the same basic strengths and weaknesses in terms of corrosion resistance and mechanical strength. The days when you could pick up a sound E-type for next to nothing are just a fond memory, and you now have a real job on your hands merely sorting out the really worthwhile cars from the overpriced rubbish. Hopefully what follows on the next few pages will make that task just a little bit easier.

Engine

All Series 1 and Series 2 E-types use the same basic XK in-line six-cylinder power unit, which was already 13 years old in 1961 and is still being used in the Daimler limousine and various military vehicles. Its last Jaguar application was with fuel injection in the Series 3 XJ6 saloon, which was replaced by an all-new model in 1986.

This amazing power unit was first seen in the show-stopping XK120 at the 1948 Earls Court Motor Show, and at the time it was just about the most advanced true production engine you could find anywhere in the world. Development of the XK engine began during the war years under Bill Heynes, Walter Hassan and Claude Baily, specifically to power a new 100mph luxury saloon that would eventually emerge in 1950 as the Mark VII. Various ideas were played around with but in the end the team came down in favour of a double overhead camshaft six-cylinder unit with a tough cast-iron block, a seven bearing crank and an aluminium cylinder head. The twin overhead camshafts were turned by separate top and bottom Reynolds duplex timing chains and operated two valves per cylinder in highly efficient hemispherical combustion chambers, developed by Harry Weslake, which promoted good exhaust valve cooling and easily controlled turbulence among other advantages. The cast-iron block was a relatively simple design with a long 106mm stroke and 83mm bore, giving a capacity of 3442cc. No liners were fitted and thanks mainly to chromium plated top rings on the alloy pistons the bores didn't wear in a hurry. The connecting rods were steel and lubrication was by a gear pump, driven, along with the distributor, off the front of the crankshaft. The end result was a very powerful engine for the day which with twin 1¾in SU carbs and 8:1 compression ratio gave 160bhp at 5000rpm and 195lb ft of torque at 2500rpm. 7:1 and 9:1 compression ratio pistons were available on request.

Not only was the XK a beautifully smooth, powerful and flexible engine to drive behind, it was also lovely to look at, with polished aluminium camshaft covers, bright aluminium inlet manifold and gloss black enamelled exhaust manifolds. These thoughtful touches have always made keeping the XK engine clean more of a pleasure than a chore.

During the fifties the engine was constantly improved and developed, mostly with an eye to even greater power, but the first really big change didn't come until 1958, when the top of the range Mark IX saloon was introduced, with a new 3.8-litre version of the unit. This variant used the B-type head on a completely new cylinder block, bored out to 87mm to give a total capacity of 3781cc, and fitted with dry liners to eliminate the cracking between cylinders which some home-grown bore-out jobs had provoked. The stated output in two-carburettor form was 220bhp. In 1959 this unit also became available in the XK150,

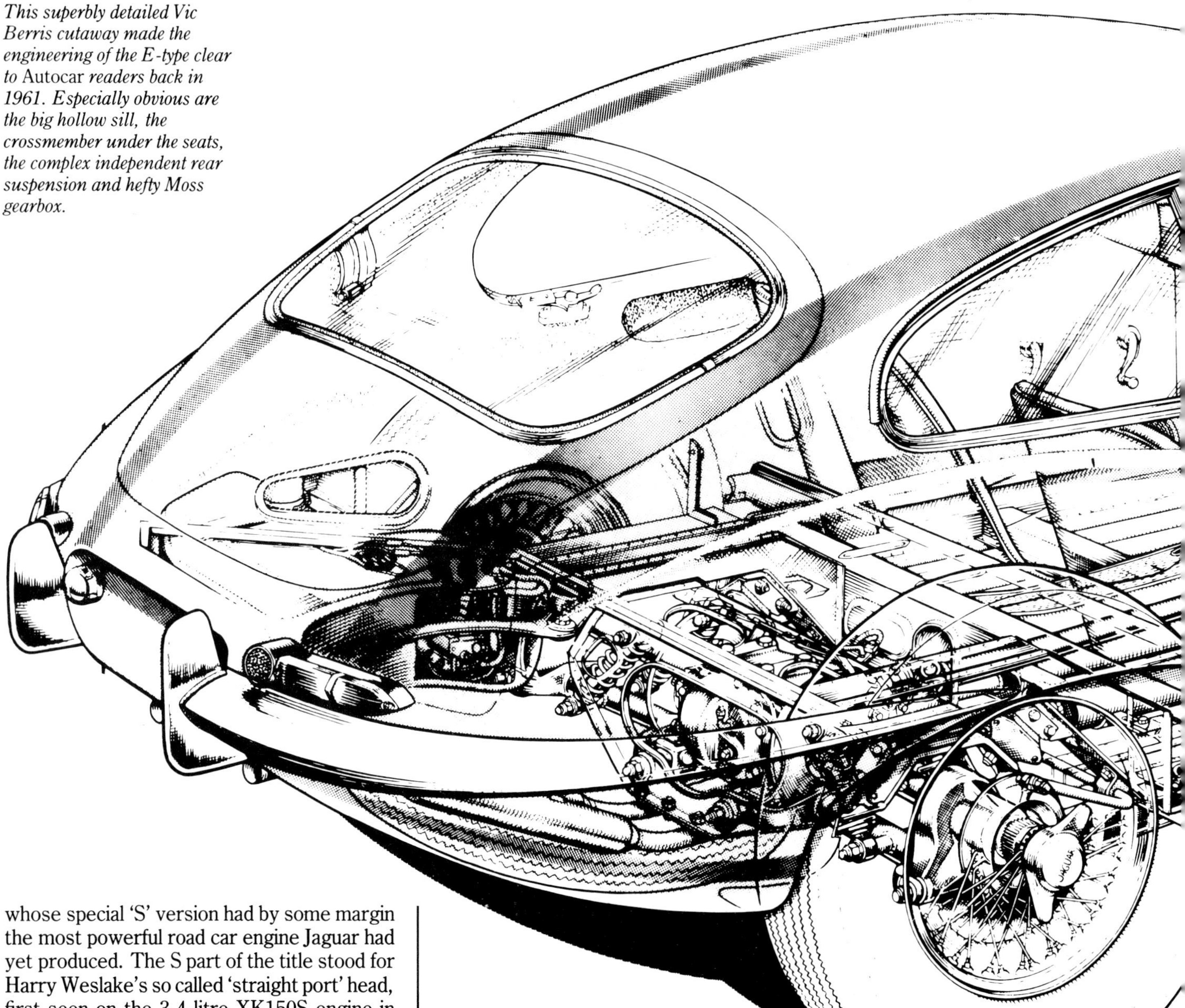

This superbly detailed Vic Berris cutaway made the engineering of the E-type clear to Autocar *readers back in 1961. Especially obvious are the big hollow sill, the crossmember under the seats, the complex independent rear suspension and hefty Moss gearbox.*

whose special 'S' version had by some margin the most powerful road car engine Jaguar had yet produced. The S part of the title stood for Harry Weslake's so called 'straight port' head, first seen on the 3.4-litre XK150S engine in 1957. Weslake had partially straightened the ports to encourage better mixture flow at high rpm, and to take advantage of this had given the engine no less than three 2in SU HD8 carbs, 9:1 compression ratio pistons, lead bronze bearings in the main and big ends, and a stronger clutch and lightened flywheel. Jaguar claimed an impressive 265bhp at 5500rpm and 260lb ft of torque at 4000rpm for the 3.8-litre XK150S, but these gross figures really have to be taken with a pinch of salt as Jaguar were having to compete with the equally exaggerated figures quoted by North American manufacturers for their huge 6½-litre-plus V8s. The engine's true net output is likely to be around 220bhp, which is impressive enough.

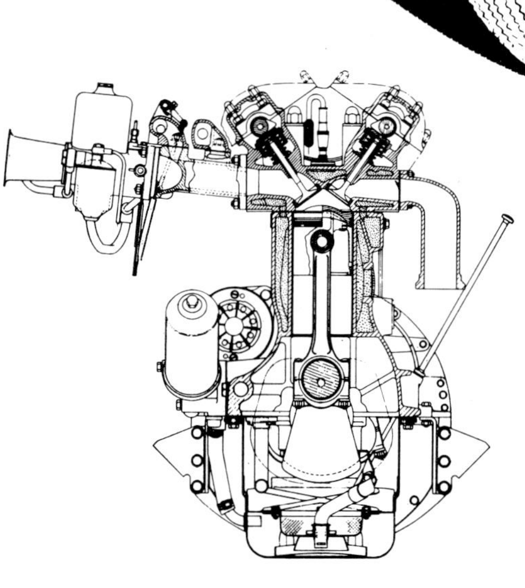

A cross-section of the XK in-line six-cylinder engine, designed principally by William Heynes.

right

The 3781cc XK engine as installed in the E-type. Like the XK150 it had the Weslake-designed 'straight port' cylinder head and three 2in SU HD8 carbs, giving an output of 265bhp (gross).

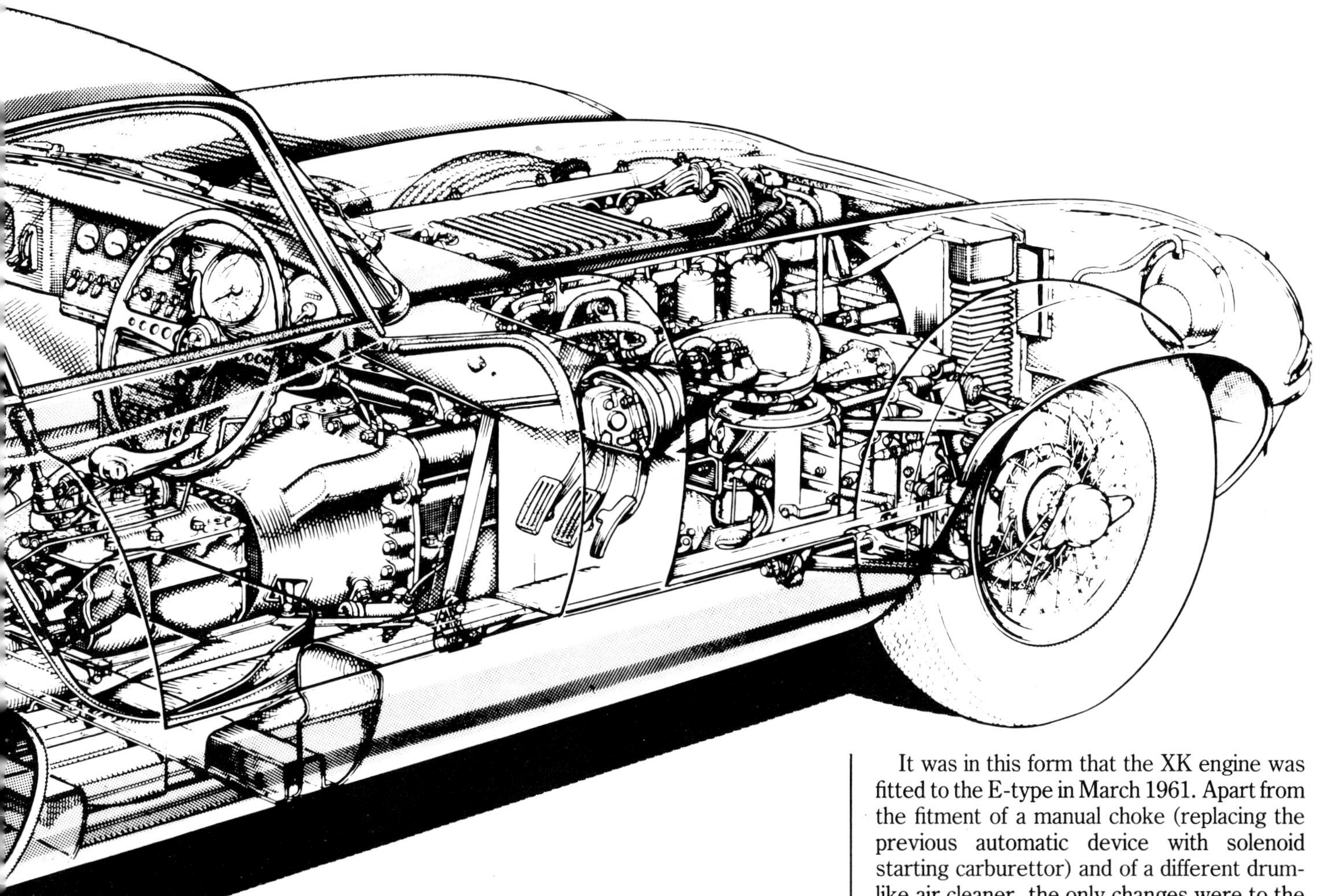

It was in this form that the XK engine was fitted to the E-type in March 1961. Apart from the fitment of a manual choke (replacing the previous automatic device with solenoid starting carburettor) and of a different drum-like air cleaner, the only changes were to the cooling system; there was a separate header tank between the radiator and engine (to reduce height) and a Lucas thermostatically controlled electrically driven fan which came in at about 80°C via a signal from the thermostat in the header tank.

The 3.8 engine served the E-type well and there's still a strong body of opinion that considers this version of the XK unit to be the nicest and most efficient of the lot. Naturally it had its problems, mostly with the linered bores flexing and allowing lubricant to by-pass the piston rings. An oil consumption of 200-300 miles per pint was usual with the 3.8 in its early years and it wasn't until June 1964 (engine number RA5649) that modified pistons with chamfers and oil drain holes below the control ring were fitted to help cure the problem. The 3.8 engine also had a habit of getting hot rather easily due to its barely adequate cooling system, with a rather feeble windscreen wiper type motor driving the fan and a none too reliable thermostat. A car stuck in traffic in very hot weather would all but boil

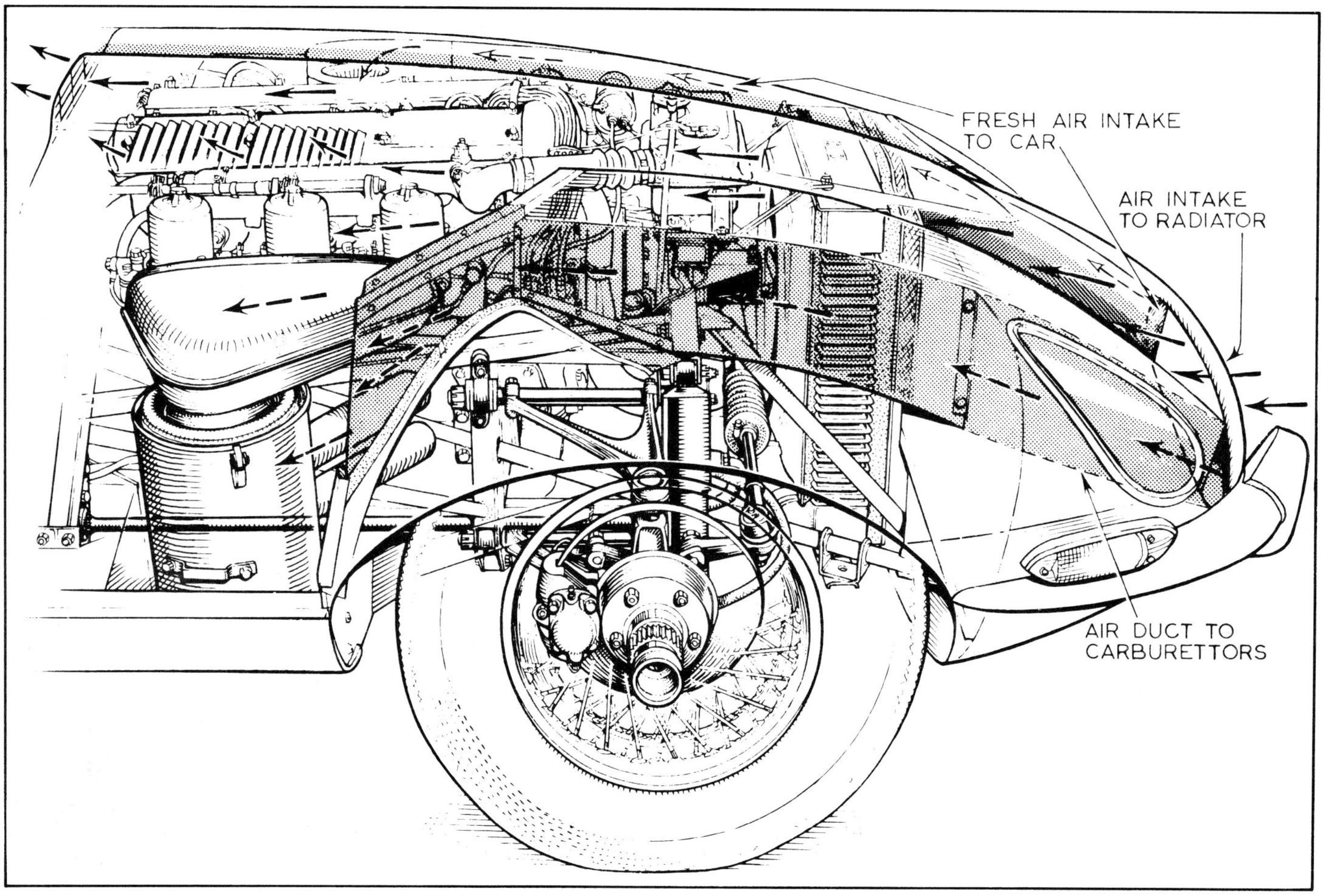

even if the system was in good order, and cockpit temperatures could thus become very uncomfortable, what with the poor insulation of the transmission tunnel and inadequate ventilation. Various modifications were made during the 3.8's production run (quick lift thermostat, higher pressure radiator cap, etc.) but the only real answer was the twin fan system introduced on the Series 2 cars in 1968.

The 4236cc engine came along in 1964 and got its greater capacity by way of a bigger 92.07mm bore, the cylinders being siamesed so that the same block size could be retained. Cylinders 2 and 5 were in the same place as before but end cylinders 1 and 6 were moved outward and 3 and 4 closer together. This meant a new crankshaft with different bearing positions, stiffer webs, altered balance weights and a torsional damper.

There was a revised inlet manifold with straighter inlet tracts, a Lucas 11AC alternator instead of a dynamo (it gave a full charge at just 910rpm), and a pre-engaged starter motor. According to Jaguar's figures the 4.2 engine gave the same power as the 3.8 (the earlier car was sold alongside the 4.2 for a short while, incidentally) but produced it at a less fussed 5400rpm. The main reason for the 4.2 was increased torque, and this went up from 260lb ft to 283lb ft at the same 4000rpm, but the bigger engine had a lower rev limit to discourage cruising above 5000rpm for long periods, which under certain rare circumstances could result in crankshaft damage. As before, 9:1 was the standard compression ratio with an 8:1 option for countries where the highest octane petrol was not available.

Changes to the 4.2-litre engine during its run in the Series 1 E-type were relatively few. From September 1966 there was a modified carb assembly and low lift cam to reduce engine speed with the choke in operation, and from around the time of the 'Series 1½' cars there was a new crossflow radiator, new water pump and the twin electric fans in angled cowls with a relay already mentioned.

The engine used in home market Series 2 E-types was little different from its predecessor, apart from less attractive ribbed cam covers, but because of federal exhaust emission regulations which came into force in 1968 North American market cars were fitted

The passage of air from the front bonnet intake to the radiator, carbs and internal ventilation filter.

right

A Forward Engineering modified engine with three Weber 45 DCOE carbs, quite a popular modification if you want more power and particularly effective in conjunction with gas-flowed heads, wilder camshaft profiles, etc., for competition use.

with just two Zenith-Stromberg carburettors with a cross-over system that ducted the mixture over the exhaust manifold, resulting in a more combustible gas that could be burnt with little residue at low engine speeds. At higher revs there was a twin throttle bypass system that allowed a more normal mixture to enter the combustion chambers. On 1969 cars a water-heated conditioning chamber replaced the cross-over, which at moderate revs warmed the mixture and sent it back to the inlet manifold. At wide throttle openings a bypass again allowed a non-heated mixture to enter the engine, but a secondary throttle plate stopped fuel condensing in the manifold and being released into the atmosphere unburnt. These modifications cut the power down to around 171bhp at 4500rpm and torque was now 230lb ft at 2500rpm, recalibrated in DIN terms.

The XK engine was a thoroughly sorted 13-year-old unit when it was first used in the E-type, and had established a reputation for strength, reliability and long life which few mass production units capable of the same power outputs could match. Any reasonably

Series 2 underbonnet scene, with ribbed cam covers, twin electric fans and a new radiator.

An emission specification Series 2 engine, with two Stromberg carbs and crossover preheating that cut power down by as much as 40bhp to 171bhp (net). This car also has air conditioning fitted, an option only available on LHD cars due to the position of the steering column.

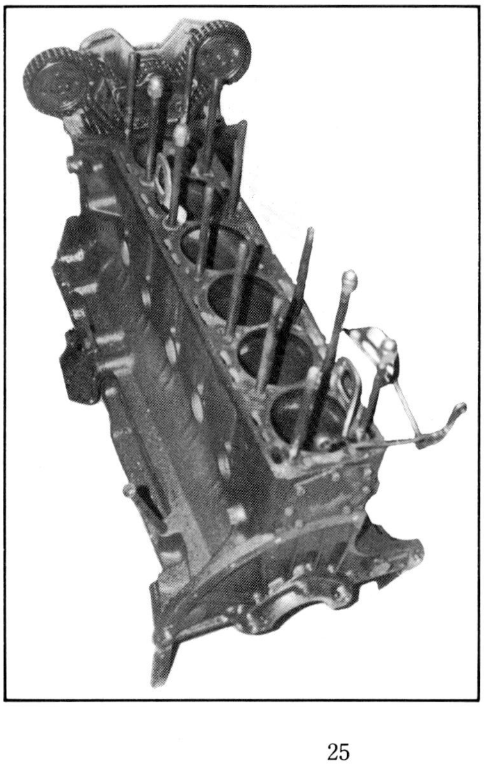

right

The XK cylinder block is one of the strongest in the business, the main rebuild problem being the sheer weight of the thing if you don't have proper lifting gear. Visible are the duplex timing chains.

well treated example should do 100,000 miles before it needs rebuilding, and with proper servicing, particularly oil changes, 200,000 miles plus is possible from one set of bearings.

To get some idea of the condition of any XK engine a road test is obviously a good idea but there are a number of things the prospective buyer can look at before the car turns a wheel. Even before starting the engine check the oil on the dipstick (located to the rear on the left) and the water in the radiator. Any indication that these two substances are mixing hints strongly at a blown head gasket. This is a fairly common complaint on the 4.2-litre cars which will lead to overheating and could mean that the thin-walled cylinder block is cracked on its top face.

If possible check the engine while still cold, as warm oil and water can make ominous internal noises, such as bearing rumble or piston slap, less easy to pinpoint. At the top end you may hear one or two noisy tappets, though the XK's valve gear should never be completely silent as this means that the tappet clearances have closed up, with possible dire consequences. On the other hand excessive noise from the cylinder head could mean wear on the tappet sleeves, buckets or valve guides, all of which is pretty expensive to have rectified. Yet another source of mechnical clatter is the timing chains; the top chain can be adjusted with a special tool when it starts to get noisy, and if worn it is quite easily replaced, but a noisy bottom chain is an engine-out job. A compression check is always a good idea.

On starting, listen to how the starter motor sounds – if it spins without turning the engine then it's possible that the pinion gear hasn't engaged or that there are broken teeth on the pinion or flywheel gears. On 4.2-litre cars with the pre-engaged starter, the roller clutch assembly has probably failed. Other starter motor problems include faulty brushes, a worn commutator or solenoid problems.

Once started the engine should tick over evenly and smoothly, anything less than this indicating out of balance carburettors or worn carburettor spindles. Other fuel supply faults can be caused by dirty contact points in the electric fuel pump or a dirty fuel filter. From cold the oil pressure gauge should start at zero and respond quickly, and it will obviously show a very good reading while the oil is still cold and thick. On the road test let the engine warm up to operating temperature (this will take a while) and then make sure that the gauge doesn't show less than 40psi at 3000rpm. Even a good reading doesn't necessarily mean that the main bearings are in good order, but a poor reading could be caused by something simple like a faulty sensor, a worn oil pump, loose oil pipes or a faulty/blocked oil pressure relief valve. On early cars the split pins that secured the locking nuts of the connecting rods to the bearing caps sometimes came adrift and caused a complete loss of pressure. Later, self-locking nuts were employed. Another cause of poor oil pressure is a blocked oil filter which is the easiest thing of all to cure. If possible, check the oil pressure gauge on the car against a mechanical one for accuracy.

As far as use of oil goes, all these engines use a fair bit by modern standards, particularly the early 3.8s, so a little blue haze under acceleration is acceptable. Obviously, clouds of blue smoke mean bore and piston ring wear, and one way of checking for this is by blipping the throttle after letting the engine idle for a minute or so after a run. Pinking is often caused by the ignition timing being too far advanced, and sometimes if the ignition is not being advanced or retarded automatically this is because the elbow joints on the advance pipe have perished or fallen off. Misfires at high revs can generally be put down to something straightforward like dirty plugs or a closed-up points gap, but don't discount something more serious like a sticking valve. A lack of oil in the carburettor piston dampers will cause poor acceleration and spitting back through the carb when the throttle is snapped open quickly. A low reading on the ammeter on dynamo equipped cars could mean a loose belt, badly worn bushes or diode failure, among other things.

If the engine overheats, a loose belt, faulty thermostat or retarded ignition could be at the root of the trouble. You can make sure that the fan motor is working by shorting out the thermostat wires. As mentioned earlier, a blown head gasket also causes the engine to overheat.

With the engine switched off and fully warm, remove the oil filler cap (which will be hot!) and look for fumes from inside and oil scum around the cap, again indicating head gasket problems or bore wear. Yet another clue to the condition of the head gasket is the coolant, which may have gone down by a pint or two after the test drive. Look also for smoke and oil fumes coming from the engine breather pipe. Oil leaks are a traditional feature of the XK unit, favourite places being from the sump gasket and cam covers.

The XK engine used in the E-type has been the motive force behind many postwar Jaguar saloons so some interchanging of parts is possible. The Mark X Jaguar was introduced in October 1961 and used virtually the same engine as the E-type with the three-carb 'S' head and 265bhp. The only major difference was the sump, which was a different shape due to the lower and more forward position of the engine in the saloon car, but with the correct sump and minor modifications to water hoses, etc., the Mark X engine can certainly be used in the E-type. The 3.8-litre Mark II and S-type saloons used a similar basic block with the two-carb B-type head, but the correct 'straight-port' 3.8 cylinder head can be fitted.

On the subject of 4.2-litre engines, the 4.2 Mark X and 420G used virtually the same unit as the 4.2-litre E-type and the two-carb units used in the 420/Daimler Sovereign and XJ6 4.2/Daimler Sovereign can be converted to E-type specification. Note that using an earlier head on a later engine (3.8S head on 4.2 block) will mean blanking out waterways in the head, and thus a later head on an earlier block will mean attention to the waterways in the block. It's also worth remembering that two types of

The three SU HD8 2in carbs fitted to the E-types, the Mark 10/420G, and 3.4 and 3.8 XK150s models. Only the E-type had a manual choke assembly.

4.2 engine were used in the XJ6, the 7L and 8L, and if you use the later 8L type in the E it will mean either putting up with a later non-standard type of oil filter assembly (on the L the cams are lubricated through a take-off on the oil filter assembly) or making up a new pipe and take-off boss to feed the camshafts as per original.

There's a minor question mark over oil filter types, too, with differences in the angle at which the filter sticks out (which can prevent the engine being fitted) and in types of oil pressure relief valve. The vertical filter assembly fitted to the earlier 8L engines fits the E, however, as does the horizontal version fitted to later XJs, both these versions having a superior later type of oil pressure relief valve and throw-away canister. Crankshafts are interchangeable between the 3.4 and 3.8 but these will not fit the 4.2 or vice versa, although cranks can be swopped among different types of 4.2 engine. Connecting rods can be swopped among all engines except the 2.4 and 2.8.

If you want to make sure that the E-type you're looking at has the engine it came out of the factory with, or at least a genuine E-type replacement, compare the engine number stamped on the right hand side of the block above the oil filter (from August '69 this was moved to the crankcase bellhousing flange on the left-hand side of the block near the dipstick) with the one on the chassis plate under the petrol filter. Prior to October 1964 the engine number prefix was R or RA and from then until October 1968 it was 7E. All Series 2 cars were designated 7R.

Gearbox

The Moss four-speed gearbox used in the 3.8 E-type goes back in essence to 1946 (well before then, in fact, if you include the pre-war version with double helical gears) and was used on the pushrod engined 1½/2½/3½ litre saloons, the Mark V and every non-automatic XK-engined Jaguar up to 1964, although the Mark II and S-type saloons carried on with the 'box until 1965. In the E-type application it had the same ratios as the XK150S, with constant-mesh synchromesh on second, third and fourth gears. The clutch was a 10-inch Borg and Beck single plate affair with hydraulic operation. This gearbox was coming in for plenty of stick long before the E-type came along, because apart from the crash first gear (which at least had a rather pleasant vintage whine) there was only weak synchromesh on the other three ratios, and if you attempted anything approaching a brisk upward or downward change (without pretty accurate double declutching) the heavy, long-travel lever grated – yet annoyingly it could sometimes go in very nicely for no apparent reason! An optional close-ratio 'box was available, with a different clutch housing, primary shaft, and oil seal.

Thankfully, with the announcement of the 4.2 E-type in 1964 Jaguar introduced a new all-synchromesh gearbox of their own design and construction, which was also fitted to the very last 3.8s. It had a cast-iron casing, positive lubrication from a pump at the rear, and inertia baulk rings that prevented engagement until the gears were properly synchronized. A Laycock 10-inch diaphragm clutch reduced the pedal movement by a useful 1½ inches. On the road this produced a far sweeter change, and you could now move the much lighter lever as quickly as you liked without beating the synchromesh, though the clutch still had to be pressed right down for really smooth changes. First still had an old fashioned whine (as did second and third to a lesser extent) and

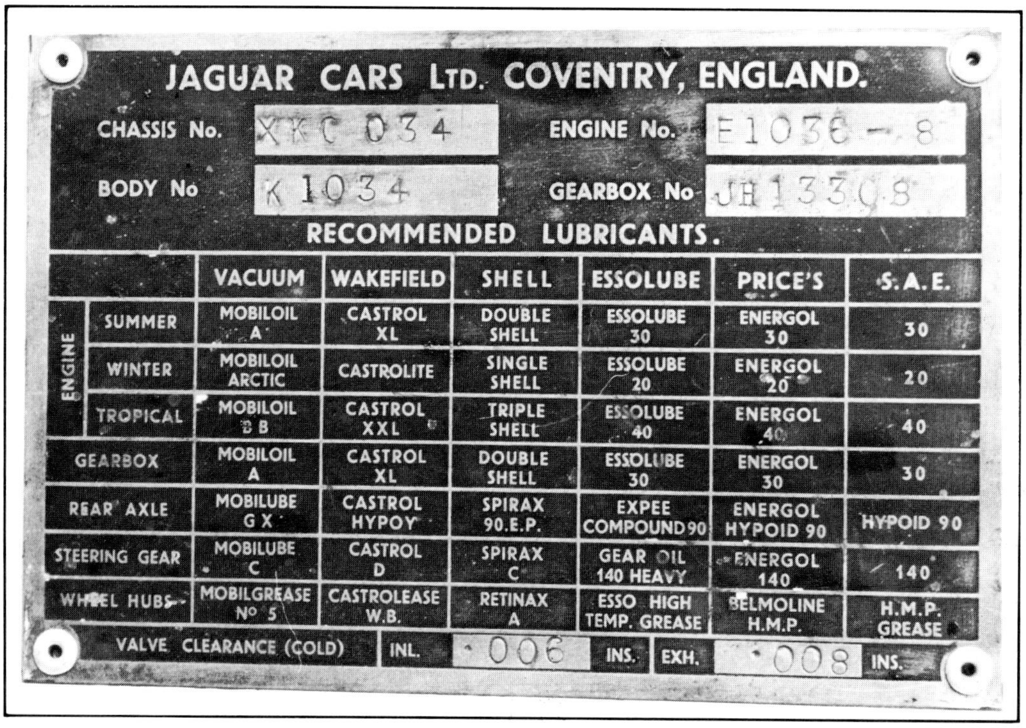

This is the E-type chassis plate located under the petrol filter in the engine compartment. By comparing the engine number on the plate with the one stamped on the right hand side of the block (on the crankcase bell housing flange from August '69) you can see if a car's engine has been replaced.

every now and again it could be a little difficult to engage from rest, though it was perfectly possible to slam the lever into bottom gear while travelling at 40mph.

One or two minor modifications were made to the all-synchromesh gearbox during its life on the E-type, such as a chamfered idler gear to reduce possible gearbox noise, and a new roller bearing fitted to the constant pinion shaft, which was later modified to include an oil thrower. In 1966 Jaguar went back to Borg and Beck for their clutches and a higher rated spring was introduced in March 1969 to reduce slipping. 2-plus-2 models had lower ratios.

So, what should you look for on the transmission front? To start with the Moss 'box is very vintage in feel, slow to use if you want crunch-free changes, and with a long lever travel. There's no synchromesh on first gear and by now there will probably be very little on the other ratios. Rough whining noises from first and reverse are normal but be suspicious of too much commotion from these gears, as this usually indicates chipped, missing or worn out teeth. Second will whine a little too but third and top should be virtually silent. The all-synchromesh Jaguar-designed 'box is also a bit noisy in first and reverse (if not to the same extent) and second whines pleasantly too, but again the noise should be in no way excessive. Test the first-gear synchro by trying to put the lever into first at about 30mph without double declutching, and see whether the synchromesh on the other ratios is effective. If the lever tends to jump out of gear then the 'box is either worn or the spring behind the striking rods locating ball is broken.

Clutches last around 40,000 miles and you can check for slippage by changing from second to top at around 25mph and applying full throttle. Hydraulic systems can also be at the root of many clutch problems, while judder is generally the fault of worn engine mountings or possibly oil on the driven plate. Another possibility is a flywheel that has been lightened too much. Worn release bearings cause annoying clunks and clicks. Finally, look for any signs of welding around the gearbox tunnel, as this means someone has done the cowboy trick of taking the gearbox out without the engine.

With the introduction of the 2-plus-2 E-type in 1966 there was the option of an automatic gearbox, in this case the well established Borg-Warner Model 8, which was imported from North America and used in cars that produced more torque than the UK-built Type 35 could safely handle. Unlike the Mark X/ 420G and 420 saloons, which also used the design, the E-type had a central T handle selector (rather than a column mounted affair) controlling L (Lock-up) and D1 and D2 ranges. It was a totally conventional design, with a torque converter coupled to a hydraulically operated planetary gearbox. In D1 the 'box ran through all the gears, while in D2 only second and top came in, which made progress

This impeccable 3.8-litre roadster was restored by its owner Dave Trueman of Wildae Restorations.

The E-type Series 1 in fixed-head coupé form.

GB 1001

Series 1 roadster and fixed-head coupé. Rear view of the coupé is particularly pleasing.

slower but smoother and more economical. There was the usual kickdown facility on the accelerator pedal so that the gearbox (in D1) would drop down from top to second below about 68mph and into bottom gear (from second or top) as long as the speed wasn't above 21mph.

Even when working correctly the Model 8 isn't the smoothest of automatic gearboxes but it is basically a robust installation. To make sure the unit is biting properly, move the selector from D to R a few times, making sure you can feel the unit engage distinctly, while a stall test – holding the gearbox against the brakes in D or R with the throttle fully depressed – will give you some idea of the condition of the gearbox and torque converter. The stall speed is the maximum speed at which the engine will drive the torque converter impeller with the turbine held stationary: normally this is 1600-1700rpm but more than about 2100 means there's slip in the clutches (or that the fluid is low) while less than 1000rpm probably means that a new torque converter is required. When doing this test don't hold the brakes on for more than 10 seconds (this causes overheating) and make sure the handbrake is applied. As always check the fluid on the dipstick. If it's black or dark in colour or gives off a horrible burnt smell then the bands have not got long to live.

As long as the ratios are correct – and remembering that the E never had overdrive – you can use gearboxes from other Jaguar models quite easily. It would be quite possible to swap your rough Moss 'box for an all-synchromesh unit, which could make a 3.8 E-type so much nicer to drive. It's also quite possible to change your automatic 2-plus-2 E-type into a manual, making the car much more pleasant to drive in terms of handling and performance and probably more valuable too, although the car will always be recognizable as being originally automatic by the extra wide transmission tunnel and BW (Borg-Warner) suffix on the chassis plate. If possible try and get hold of the original 2-plus-2 manual 'box with the long tail shaft, or a non-overdrive XJ6 'box, although as both these are quite rare you may have to settle for a normal short chassis E-type gearbox or one from an S-type, Mark II or 420. You *can* fit overdrive but this means altering the rear mounting, the propshaft length and the propshaft tunnel to accommodate the extra length. With a short-chassis gearbox six inches will have to be added to the propshaft anyway, and there will be complications around the tunnel cover, which is much bigger on the automatic and doesn't have a removable lid. You will need the correct 2-plus-2 manual centre console too.

Suspension, steering and brakes

The front suspension of the E-type was designed along traditional Jaguar lines and was basically a development of the system used on the D-type racing car. Slim forged wishbones were used top and bottom (with upper and lower ball pivots) and the bottom wishbone was anchored each side of the car to a longitudinal torsion bar, which was attached under the scuttle assembly. Metalastic inner wishbone mountings were provided, plus inclined telescopic dampers at each side and an anti-roll bar connected to the outer ends of each lower wishbone. It was a sound, well proven design that was to give little trouble over the years.

Hardly any British cars had independence at the rear end in 1961 (and continental models so equipped often didn't handle well) so Jaguar's first such design for the E-type generated a great deal of interest when details were released. Designed under the auspices of William Heynes, the layout used a pressed steel bridge-type subframe carrying the whole suspension assembly plus the differential, hub carriers and the inboard disc brakes, all of which were very effectively isolated from the main body by four bonded rubber mountings. The only suspension parts outside the subframe were the two trailing radius arms, which provided longitudinal location for the subframe, and these, along with the anti-roll bar attached to the lower links, were rubber mounted, so there was no metal-to-metal contact in the suspension. The design worked on the double wishbone principle, although the upper link was actually a fixed-length, double universal jointed driveshaft running into big aluminium hub carriers. The carriers were attached to the lower transverse tubular links, and springing was by two coil spring/damper units on either side, the idea behind this being that each individual unit could be made smaller than one large one on either side, saving installation space. They were attached to the lower wishbone on projecting lugs and to the top of the subframe. A Salisbury 4HU Hypoid final drive was used with a Powr-Lok limited slip differential as standard. This latter unit – with replaceable multiplate clutches – provided traction to whichever of the rear wheels was getting more adhesion than the other, rather than letting it through the spinning wheel.

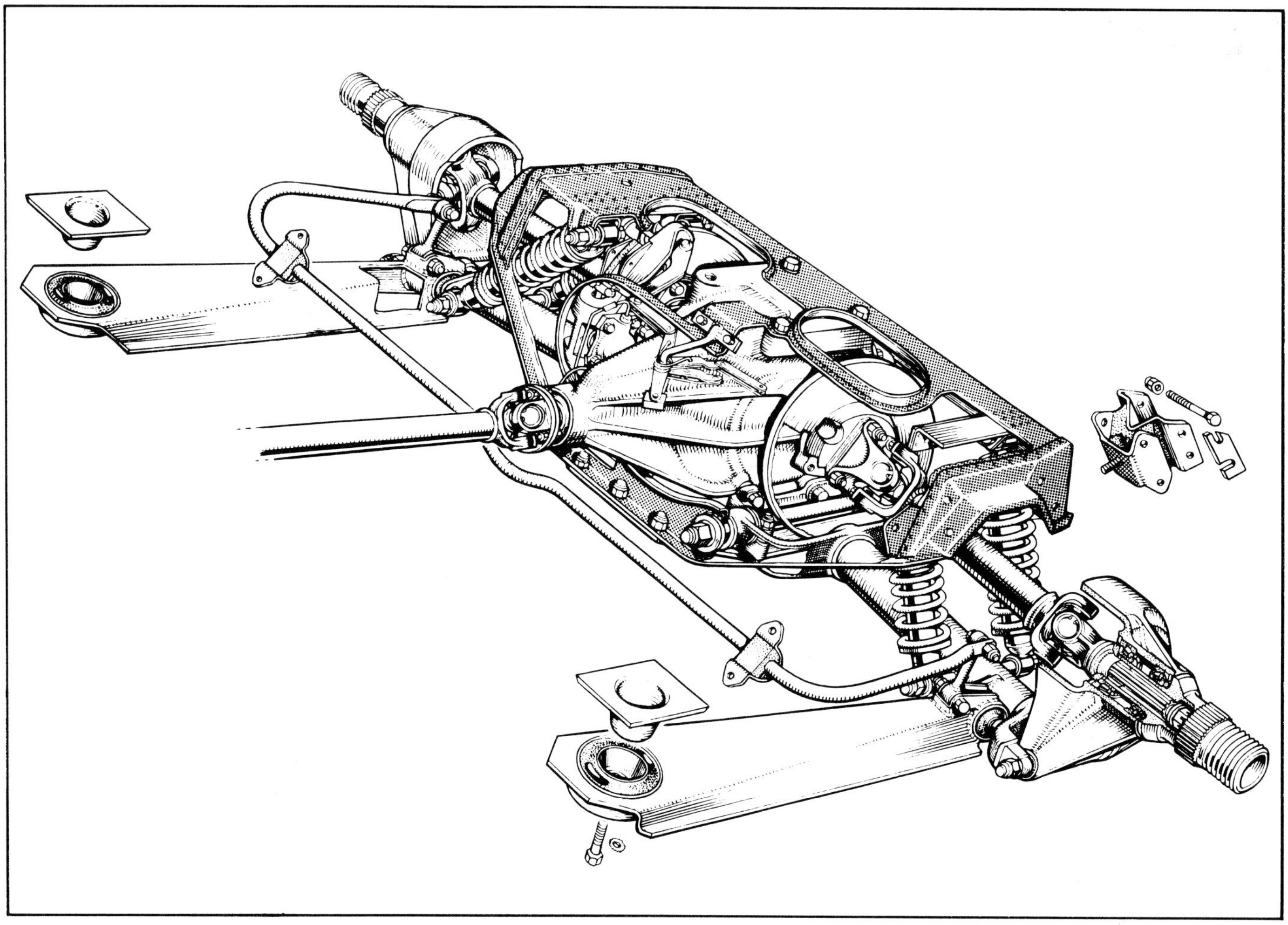

The E-type's independent rear suspension, showing the big steel subframe with central Salisbury diff, inboard Dunlop disc brakes and four spring damper units. At the outer ends of the drive shafts are the big aluminium hub carriers, with the radius arms extending from the bottom wishbone.

Just a word about axle ratios. The standard European market axle ratio when the E-type first appeared was 3.31:1(2.93, 3.07 and 3.54 were the alternatives) but before long Jaguar were swopping and changing ratios with great frequency. The 3.07:1 final drive became standard in the UK in October 1962, the 2.93:1 option was dropped, and North American and Canadian market cars got the 3.31:1 ratio, which was changed 11 months later to 3.54! E-types exported to the USA always had lower (numerically higher) final drive ratios because acceleration was felt to be more important there than top speed, hence the brilliant standing start acceleration and quarter mile times of US test E-types. British market 4.2 Series 1 E-types went back to 3.07:1 in April 1965. Automatics only came with a 2.88:1 ratio.

So good were the front and rear suspension systems of the E that very few changes were made. Early on the 3.8 car got longer rear road springs and solid forged halfshafts with sealed-for-life joints, while Series 1 4.2 models received polyurethane seals on the front suspension (increasing servicing intervals on the ball joints from 2500 to 12,000 miles), and stiffer rear road springs to prevent bottoming, although later 3.8s had actually been given spacers to achieve the same effect. The Powr-Lok limited slip differential became optional in September 1967 (it wasn't an integral part of the final drive unit) except on North American market cars with the 3.54:1 axle ratio.

Ball joints are the usual problem with the front suspension, and you can check for play by levering the wheel up with a bar while it is suspended and looking at how much drop the ball joint allows. Make sure the torsion bars are not bent and see if the car sits low at the front; if it does the torsion bars may need adjusting, which isn't as simple a job as it sounds. Dry grease nipples hint at a lack of proper maintenance.

The rear suspension is much more complex and thus presents more potential snags. On the road there should be no bottoming, rear wheel steering, instability or wallowing on corners, any of these traits indicating worn

One of the big problems with the E-type's rear suspension is that maintenance is awkward. Unless you know what you're doing, most jobs – even replacing the brake pads – mean dropping the whole unit.

springs/dampers (there are four of each, don't forget) or deterioration of the Metalastic mountings holding the subframe to the body.

Clonking from the rear end can usually be traced to worn universal joints, the bottom pivot bearings of the rear stub axle carrier or possibly the stub axle splines. You can check all this by jacking the rear end up and looking for play in these components. Some play in the wheel bearings is acceptable but there must be none whatsoever in the all-important universal joints on the driveshafts, which you can check by trying to twist the shaft against the hub. The differential could well be leaking, possibly due to simple overfilling or a blocked breather, or from the seals because of the heat generated by the nearby inboard disc brakes. A lack of oil causes the unit to distort and overheat. A clicking from the back end when accelerating on full lock indicates that the limited-slip components in the differential are doing their intended job. There should be virtually no axle whine.

The E-type's highly rated steering was a rack and pinion system, the rack running behind the radiator and connected to the steering wheel by a universally jointed adjustable steering column. It was geared for 2½ turns lock to lock and allowed a turning circle of about 35½ feet. A seven-tooth pinion was introduced in May 1966 to improve the steering on cars fitted with radial tyres and when the Series 2 was introduced in 1968 there was the option of Adwest power steering, a system incorporating the assistance mechanism from a Marles Bendix peg and cam with the Alford and Adler rack and pinion. Series 2 cars also got a steering column lock. There shouldn't be any free play in the steering, although the rack may move slightly on its rubber mountings. If the steering is loose suspect worn universal joints in the column or a worn spline. The rack and its rubber mountings frequently wear, and stiff steering suggests a lack of lubrication. Check the rubber gaiters on the steering rack and look for play in the track rod ends.

The 3.8 E-type used Dunlop self-adjusting disc brakes, with two cylinders on each wheel, twin master cylinders and separate hydraulic circuits. An unusual feature was the American Kelsey Hayes 'bellows' servo, which augmented the load applied to the brake pedal (via a balance bar) in direct proportion to the effort applied by the driver. Built under licence by Dunlop, this mechanical booster was not a complete success, as its response was somewhat delayed and the boost pressure tended to change suddenly, causing some E-type owners to unintentionally 'redesign' the front of the long bonnet. At the front 11in discs were used, with 10in items at the rear, these being mounted inboard and acting directly on the driveshafts. Being in such an enclosed position the rear discs were short of cooling air and could get very hot indeed when used hard. In fact fade was quite easily induced with these brakes, and the E didn't really get a braking system that matched its performance until the advent of the Series 3. The handbrake was non-self-adjusting at first, but from October 1961 there was a self-adjusting ratchet mechanism with its own calipers, although this was always a marginal arrangement.

Jaguar must have been sensitive to criticism of the E-type's brakes because they seemed to be under constant revision, with modified master cylinders in January 1962, modified pedal and power lever in May of that year, and thicker ½in rear discs with new calipers in June 1963, plus half a dozen other minor improvements up to the introduction of the 4.2 model in 1964. This car got a far more satisfactory Lockheed vacuum booster, a vacuum valve on the master cylinder (which was still attached directly to the brake pedal lever) transmitting the response from the pedal over to the remote servo unit via the dual lines. Though the discs could still glow bright red on a fast Alpine descent, at least

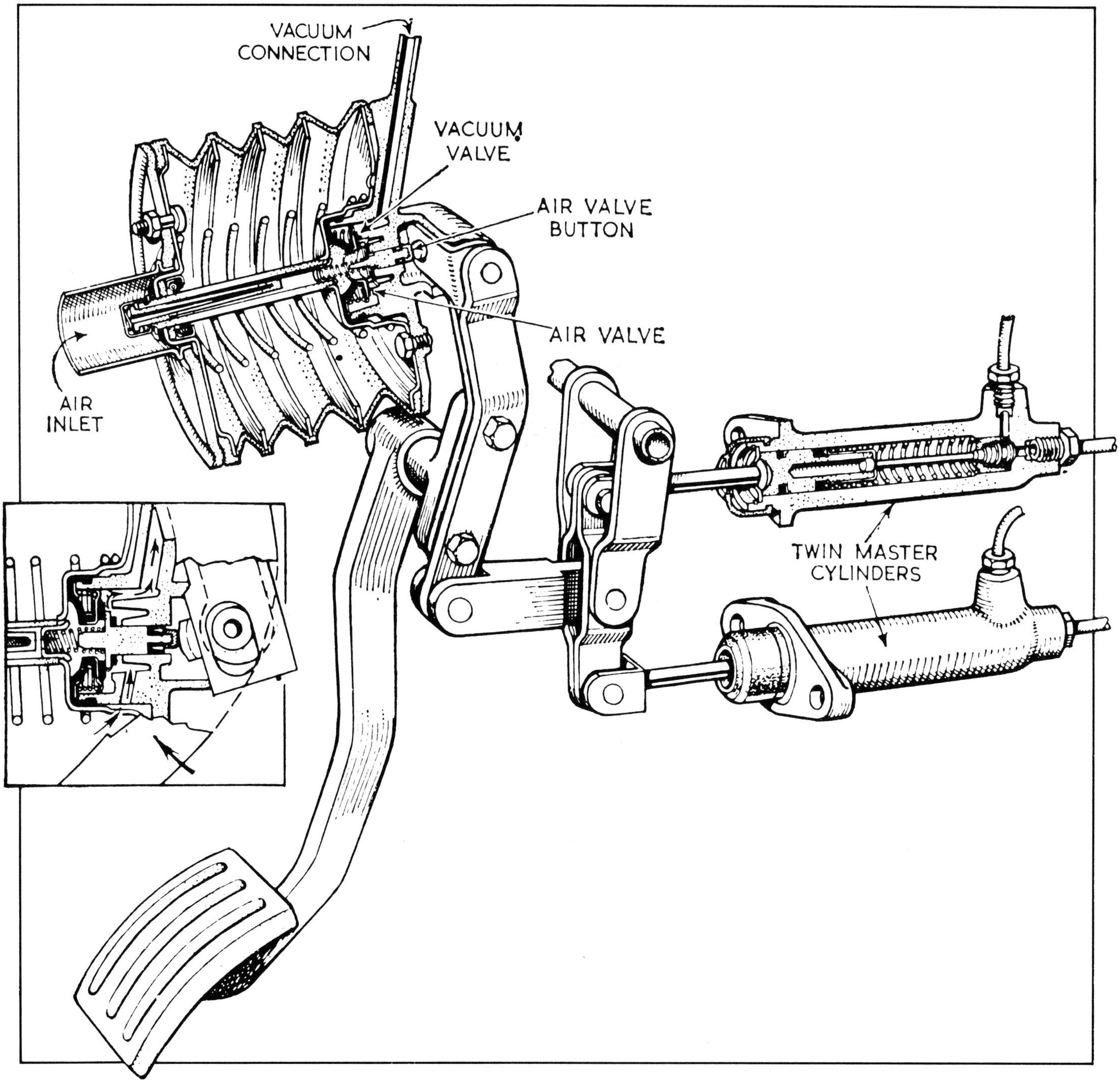

pedal effort was much reduced and there was also better progression, making town driving and parking a less heart-stopping experience. The Series 2 E-types used Girling disc brakes, the 11.8in front discs having a bigger rubbed area thanks to three-pot calipers, with two small cylinders on one side of the caliper and one large cylinder on the other.

The braking system of the E-type can give plenty of problems, particularly the Dunlop-built set-up, which seems to suffer more if not used for long periods of time. The discs themselves glaze, score and warp, causing judder, pulling and wobble problems that can set the car and driver dangerously off balance during hard driving. Calipers seize up, pads rust into their calipers and of course leaks are commonplace, due to worn rubbers in the brake and master cylinders; changing those rear inboard brake seals is no easy task, either . . . A spongy pedal will mean air in the system, or perhaps worn caliper pistons, while lengthy pedal travel is generally the fault of worn pads or a low fluid level.

Kelsey-Hayes mechanical brake booster (built under licence by Dunlop) fitted to the 3.8 E-type, which applied a mechanical pressure to twin master cylinders.

One aspect of the E-type we haven't talked about yet is the wheels. On the Series 1 cars, chromed or grey painted Dunlop 15in 72-spoke wire wheels were used, with 5in rims and centre lock hubs. The standard tyres were Dunlop RS 6.40 x 15 crossplies, although by October 1965 Dunlop SP41 radials had become standard. You could order Dunlop R5 racing tyres for your 3.8 E-type incidentally, of 6.00 section at the front and 6.50 section at the rear, and these came on so called competition wire wheels, the back pair having a rim half an inch wider than normal. On the Series 1 the hubs and spokes were strengthened, and bland looking chromium plated pressed steel wheels were offered as an option. By the end of 1969 all markets used the non-eared hub caps on the wire wheels that had originally only been used on German and American export models. Most cars are fitted with wire wheels, and these need to be checked for loose spokes and rust. Listen for clunks as the drive is taken up as this could well mean worn splines.

The scope for making do with parts off lesser Jaguars in the suspension, steering and braking departments is fairly limited. Certain front suspension items from the compact saloons can be fitted to the E, such as the stub axles, but at the rear very little can be used because driveshaft lengths vary and the E-type's irs uses an anti-roll bar. However, as long as the ratio is appropriate and a limited slip device is fitted, final drive units can be swopped quite freely. Braking systems can also be swopped about, and if you use your 3.8 regularly (and don't mind a little non-originality) it would be well worth fitting the 4.2 booster or even going over to the complete Series 2 Girling system which is much better and more reliable. However, it's worth remembering that the correct uprights have to be used if you change your braking system over. On a car as valuable and as fast as the E-type it's always advisable to use new parts in the steering, suspension and brakes.

Body

The E-type's styling and engineering were inspired directly by the D-type racing car. It was largely the work of the brilliant Malcolm Sayer, with some artistic input from Sir William Lyons himself. The E-type's 'chassis' was basically made up of two halves. The main part, running from the front bulkhead rearwards, was a stressed skin section forming the passenger compartment (and carrying the rear suspension) made up largely of 20 gauge steel panels, while forward of this monocoque 'tub' was a detachable framework of Reynolds 5H square section tubing carrying the engine and front suspension.

Two deep hollow sills running each side of the monocoque provided the main strength, going as far as the wheels at the front end and terminating at the rear where they met a hollow transverse member just forward of the rear suspension. Flitch plates 10 inches wide ran diagonally from outer top to inner bottom at four points inside the sills where the front

Exploded view of the E-type's construction, showing the monocoque centre section with its strong but rot-inducing box sections and the front subframe tubing.

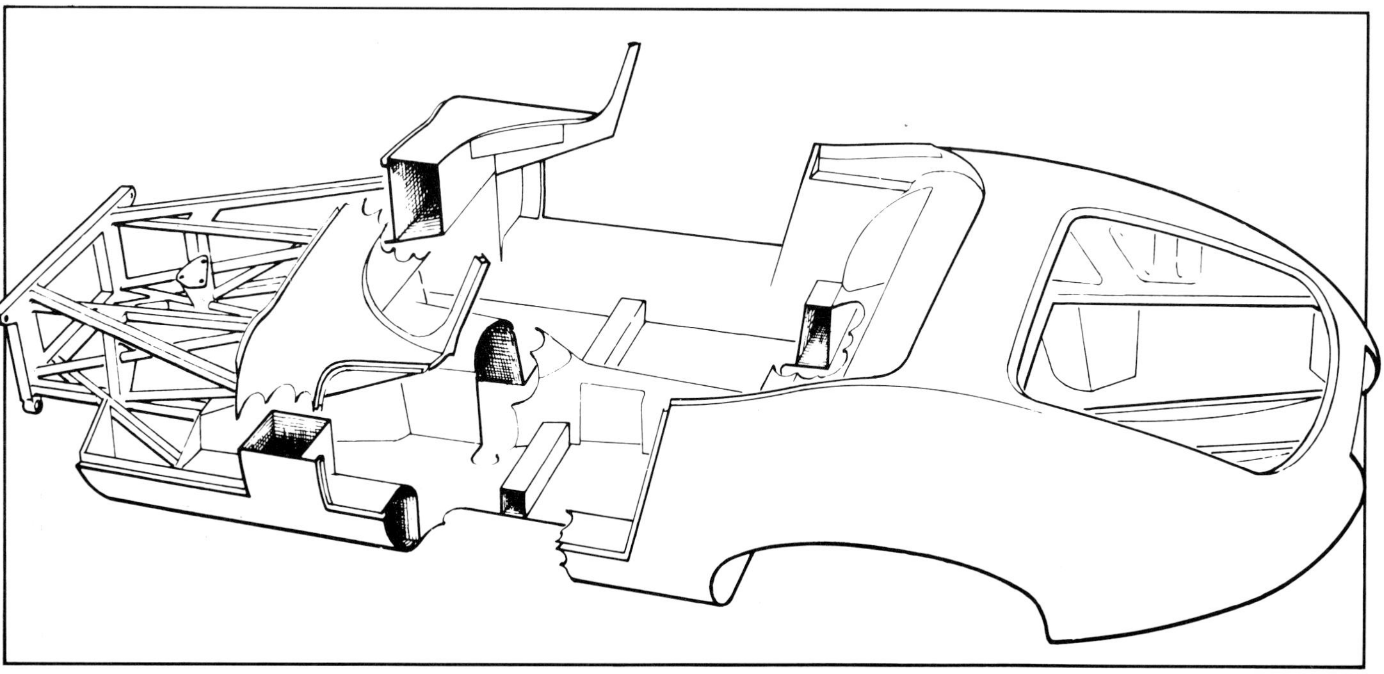

85

left

The roadster looked good with the hood up and the top itself was easy to raise and fairly watertight, although wind noise was always a problem.

below

Twelve lightweight cars were built between March 1963 and January 1964, everything possible being made in aluminium. These had a 300bhp-plus alloy-block 3.8-litre Lucas-injected XK engine with dry sump lubrication, and many other mods, such as a boot lid ventilation slot to help get rid of heat from the rear inboard brakes.

below right

Most E-types had their registration numbers stuck on the bonnet but for some foreign markets the plate had to be mounted underneath on a hinge mechanism that tilted it back when the bonnet was raised. As shown here, some British owners took up the idea.

and rear bulkheads met the sills. The scuttle and bulkhead were formed by two vertical box sections that rose from the sills with dog leg hollow extensions projecting backwards at each side at the top to the windscreen side pillars. Further strength was provided by the steel flooring, transmission hump and propshaft tunnel, and there was also a square section transverse member running across the floor under the seats. Providing the main strength for the rear suspension assembly was a low bulkhead behind the seats joining the sills. Welded to the boot floor and inner wheel arches were arched box members running from the rear bulkhead to hold the suspension cradle. Internally the rear bulkhead was strengthened by five boxes on either side of the transmission tunnel to take the strain of the suspension's two trailing radius arms. The coupé's roof provided further strength but so rigid was the structure that the roadster model needed no further bracing.

Bolted onto this structure (at six attachment points) was the front subframe, which as mentioned was built up of Reynolds square section tubing with further tubular bracing. The main section carried the engine and front suspension torsion bar anchorages, and onto it was bolted a further smaller framework carrying the radiator and bonnet pivots. The major part of the subframe could be further stripped down into three separate pieces, comprising the two side members and the square front crossmember or 'picture frame'.

The big front-hinged bonnet was unstressed and made in three detachable parts, these being the main centre section and wings either side, the joins hidden by chrome finishers. The centre section had louvres either side and a power bulge which finished in a vent underneath the windscreen. Early cars had louvres made of separate sheets of metal let into the bonnet but they were later pressed straight into the panel. The beautifully integrated light units were covered by the famous toughened glass covers, which didn't do much for lighting performance (the spread was insufficient at high speeds) but looked great! The bonnet was held down by Budget locks on very early cars (internal locking handles were used later) and was counterbalanced by coil springs when lifted, giving superb access to the engine compartment.

In the coupé, access to the luggage compartment was through a rear door hinged on the left, and on the roadster via a normal lift-up lid. In both cases these were opened from the passenger compartment. The roadster had very restricted luggage space (although there was a small stowage area behind the seats), but the fixed-head had quite a reasonable luggage platform with a hinged flap to prevent luggage flying around. Under the Hardura matting and wooden floorboard were the spare wheel and toolkit, while to the

Rear end of a Series 1 4.2 roadster, showing the tapering bumpers and slim Lucas tail lamps as used on the 3.8. Tail lamps are not interchangeable between roadsters and coupés as their rear ends were contoured differently.

left of these was another floorboard covering the kidney shaped fuel tank, which was rubber mounted to prevent drumming. The doors were not directly interchangeable between the open and closed models and the roadster had a piece of trim along the top edge not fitted to the fixed-head. The E-type was pleasingly restrained in chrome embellishment, with slim, tapering bumpers (fitted with overriders front and rear), an unobtrusive decorative bar inside the air intake and minimal chrome round the windows and headlights. Neat light units were used at the rear and these differed very slightly between open and closed models due to the former's more gently curving rump. The lightly wrapped-round front windscreen had no less than three windscreen wipers linked in unison and operated by a two-speed motor. A heated rear window was optional on the fixed-head at first.

The E-type's outer curved body panels, including the bonnet, were built by Abbey Panels, and Pressed Steel Fisher produced the inner sections, the whole lot then being welded up and lead loaded at Browns Lane.

Beautiful as the E-type undoubtedly was, Jaguar seem to have forgotten that people of all shapes and sizes would be driving the car and by the closing months of 1961 complaints about the lack of leg room had led to the introduction of proper footwells in the cockpit floor and a semi-circular indentation riveted on behind the driver's seat to allow for more rearward adjustment. Later, in June 1962, a new rear bulkhead pressing was introduced, with proper pressed-in indentations on both the driver's and passenger's sides. Internal bonnet catches came along in September 1961, replacing the external Budget locks and curing bonnet shake problems. From then on very little of any importance changed on the Series 1 cars body-wise, but from March 1966 there was a major new version of the E-type for people who had to carry a small family or occasionally needed more room: the 2-plus-2.

At 15ft 4½in the 2-plus-2 was nine inches longer than the standard fixed-head coupé, the extra length being in the centre tub, which also meant that the doors were wider by some 8½ inches. The windscreen was taller by 1½ inches, which gave more headroom but increased the frontal area by 5%. The whole point of the exercise was to give room for the small bench rear seat, which was mounted on a revised rear bulkhead that had been moved back and made lower. Luggage capacity was increased and there was more front seat adjustment, so now almost anyone could squeeze into an E-type and be reasonably comfortable. This bodyshell also allowed room for a bigger transmission tunnel to fit the automatic gearbox Americans had wanted for so long, and there was a better heat shield between the exhaust and floor, which reduced cockpit temperatures. Because of the rather upright look of the windscreen the 2-plus-2 wasn't as elegant as the standard wheelbase car but it was exactly the sort of E-type the

The 2-plus-2 E-type was introduced in 1966. Its wheelbase was nine inches longer and it had a higher roofline to accommodate the small rear seats.

American market had been crying out for since the beginning, and in fact it accounted for nearly half of all closed Series 1 4.2 production.

Although Jaguar didn't admit to it at the time, a sort of interim E-type was phased into production during the closing months of 1967, known (retrospectively) as the 'Series 1½'. This car took on board many Series 2 features during its production run before Jaguar went the whole hog with the fully revised model in October 1968, most notably the less attractive but much more effective open-style headlights, although other aspects of the car's bodywork remained as before.

Modifications to the body of the Series 2 proper were much more extensive, and not always for the better. Those open light units – which knocked two or three mph off the top speed – were brought forward in the wings by two inches and mounted in thicker looking chrome surrounds, while that beautiful, pouting air intake was increased in area by 68% to improve cooling and get a bigger volume of air to the air conditioning system that was now optional on left hand drive cars. A more clumsy looking central decorative bar came too. The bumpers were raised slightly, the rear one continuing right over the new style square number plate, while the rear lights were now much bigger, rectangular affairs mounted beneath rather than above the bumper bar. Twin reversing lights were fitted, and because the number plate was mounted lower the exhaust tail pipes were now splayed either side. The bigger front side lights and flasher units were also mounted beneath the bumper. On the 2-plus-2 the screen rake angle was increased from 46½ to 53½ degrees by bringing the base of the

The windscreen of the Series 1 2-plus-2 always looked a little upright because of the higher roofline, so on the Series 2 the base of the screen was brought forward almost to the bonnet, increasing the rake angle from 46½ degrees to 53 degrees. This left room on the scuttle for only two wipers.

left

Autocar's *Jeff Daniels enjoying himself in a Series 2 2-plus-2.*

top right

The 2-plus-2 in Series 2 form, the most practical six-cylinder E-type if not the most desirable.

right

The comparatively rare Series 2 coupé, of which only 4800 were built.

screen forward, nearer the bonnet, to give the car's screen a less upright look. This also meant that the Series 2 2-plus-2 didn't have the usual three windscreen wipers as there was no longer enough room under the scuttle.

The Jaguar E-type probably rates as one of the rot boxes of all time and generally speaking rust can break out almost anywhere, although as many people have found to their cost it is relatively easy to disguise a rotten car with liberal applications of body filler and a nice flashy spray job.

The logical place to start looking for problems is the bonnet panel, because although this structure is unstressed and doesn't affect the E-type's strength it does account for the best part of half the car's length and rusts quite prolifically. The flanges between the bolt-on wings and the main centre section generally begin to show problems first, so there may be some fairly obvious giveaways like paint bubbles or rust pimples either side of the chrome trim, or a wavy, uneven look to this area all the way along, indicating filler, and of course you can test for this with a magnet. You can confirm any suspicions by opening the bonnet and prodding the flange from the inside with a screwdriver. Rust bubbles around the wheel arches and around the bottoms of the headlamps are quite common, and inside the bonnet you could well find rust on the bulkhead that surrounds the headlamp bowl. There's a sort of flitch plate behind the wheels that catches mud, and this also tends to corrode. The nose of the bonnet is very vulnerable and will almost certainly have been bumped at some time and repaired with filler, so check it with a magnet. Feel inside the air intake for signs of rust too. Quite advanced corrosion can often be found on the bonnet hinge mounting crossmember at the front.

Because of their shape it's virtually impossible to repair existing bonnet sections effectively, so it's often a toss-up between buying new wings or a complete new bonnet. Generally, despite the seemingly high cost, a new bonnet is the sensible solution. No matter how sound the centre section seems there's always more rot around the flanges than you think and you can often end up paying almost as much to have the repairs carried out as a new factory bonnet would have cost! You can also reclaim some of your money by selling your old bonnet, as there always seems to be a healthy demand for them. As you might expect, good rot-free secondhand bonnets are rare.

Move on now to the subframe tubing. This structure is quite tough as far as corrosion resistance goes and usually suffers at the hands of people who jack the car up in the wrong place, often under the 'picture frame' area at the front, thus damaging the radiator as well. Accident damage is another possibility, so look for poorly executed repairs and bent tubes. Stress cracks are often found around the flanges at the bulkhead ends, and any of the brazed joints is susceptible to cracking. Internal corrosion of the tubes is possible, and you may also find rust on the

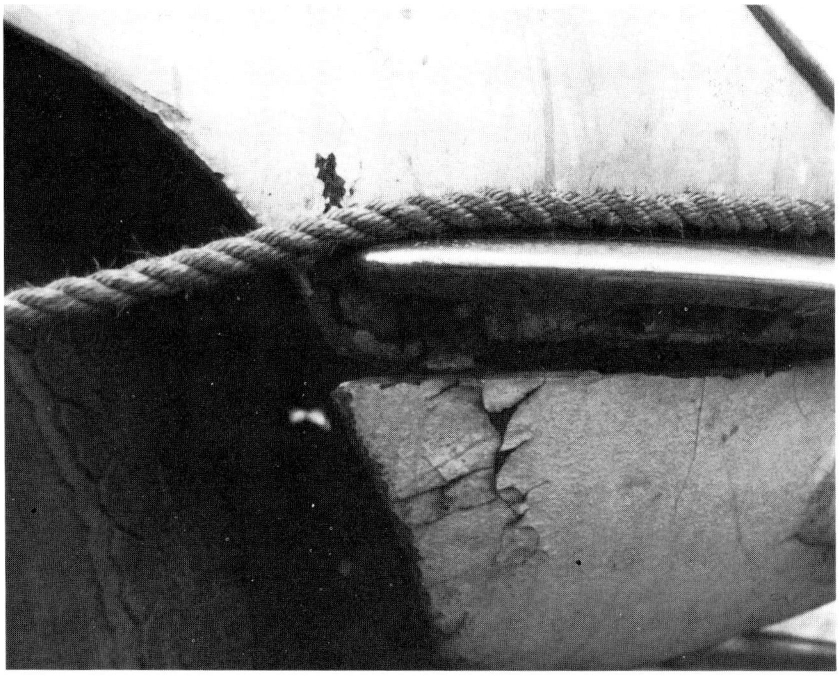

above

Rot has attacked the front panel under the bumper on this Series 2.

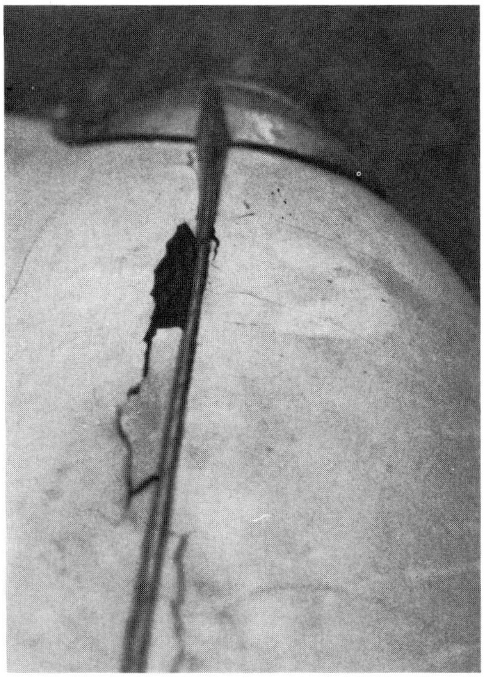

left

The bonnet rots in numerous areas, most commonly along the flange between the centre section and outer wings. It is very hard to repair this kind of damage properly and the best solution is always a new bonnet.

top

Rust in the headlamp well, where water tends to gather.

top right

Don't forget to check the air intake for rot and filler, as this part of the car often suffers minor accident damage.

right

The vital lower subframe mounting point, visible with the battery or airbox removed. Corrosion like this means a major rebuild.

bottom right

This is how the mounting point looks with the tubes removed. Check the rest of the bulkhead for corrosion and for distortion due to accident damage.

exposed lower members of the subframe. Repairing a subframe is very much an expert's job and generally it's better (and safer) to replace the whole frame than repair or replace it in sections. New frames are available but costly.

It's also important to check the front bulkhead for distortion. This points to hefty accident damage at some point in the car's history, the subframe being pushed back into the bulkhead by the impact and quite probably twisting the whole monocoque. Obviously a car like this, especially if it is being sold as a runner, is best avoided if you want to save yourself a lot of grief. A major rebuild is on the cards if the section of the bulkhead that can be seen under the bonnet is going rotten, corrosion here usually starting where the lower subframe members are mounted on either side. You can only examine these areas effectively by removing the battery and air cleaner box mounted on the left and right hand sill extensions forward of the bulkhead. Outwardly the bulkhead/scuttle section between the bonnet and windscreen almost always corrodes where it joins the outer sill, although this usually isn't very evident and can be covered with filler many times over the years before a car is stripped down for

These two shots show the effects of incorrect jacking under the E-type's subframe. At the front the car should only be jacked under the wishbone inner pivots.

restoration, so check this with your trusty magnet.

The central monocoque or 'tub' of the E-type is crucial to the car's strength and safety and is easily the most expensive and time consuming part of the car to restore. It rusts so freely because it is made up of numerous closed, welded-up box sections which let moisture and condensation in but cannot get rid of it effectively. Thus, unbeknown to owners, the E-type rusted from the inside outwards, this process being quickened in the already damp British climate by the use of salt on the roads in winter. Needless to say, Jaguar's rust proofing methods were nothing more than perfunctory during this period.

The two hollow sills running the length of the monocoque on either side are the most important check points and you will be hard pressed to find a car outside California that has not had the outer covers replaced at least twice by now. Unless filler has been used I fancy you will not have any trouble spotting rust on the outer sills, the first signs being pimples along the bottom or possibly big holes, indicating problems all the way along where the sill joins the footwell, the sections of the floorpan either side and around the jacking points. Also check the sill ends inside the rear wheel arches and the sill extensions under the bonnet, the one on the left hand (battery) side being particularly rot-prone due to acid spillage. Any problems you can see on the outer sills, no matter how small, almost always mean that there will be real carnage inside, but checking the inner sills is not so easy because they are covered by vinyl trim sections inside the car and most vendors are not particularly keen to let you remove them. So if the outer sills appear sound but you want to satisfy yourself that all is well inside, press your fingers hard against the very bottom of the inner sill where it joins the floor; if there is any give, then the inner sills are rotten. Trim panels either side of the door opening can be removed to give further visual access to the inner sills and to the lower part of the door post, which also rots. 2-plus-2 models tend not to suffer quite so badly as they have a slightly better sill-to-floor configuration. The floor can rot in all sorts of areas, but particularly where it meets the sill. Look for crude looking repairs or maybe even false panels.

A good way to check the rigidity of an E-type – especially a roadster – is to jack the car up on the chassis rail in the centre and then examine the door gap, which will have opened up somewhat towards the top if the car is bending in the middle, indicating a rotten structure.

Some E-types have problems with water retention around the windscreen seals but you don't find the corrosion that results until the windscreen is removed. Rot at the base of the screen pillar is another common problem, and coupés are sometimes rusty underneath the piece of chrome trim at the top of the pillar. The top of the door aperture is also worth a check.

If anything, the rear half of the 'tub' offers even more potential horrors. The rear bulkhead is a particular danger point, corrosion showing itself in the five essential

The subframe tubes rot from the inside and repairs like this one are not recommended. Replacing the whole subframe is the only proper solution as the rot never confines itself to one area.

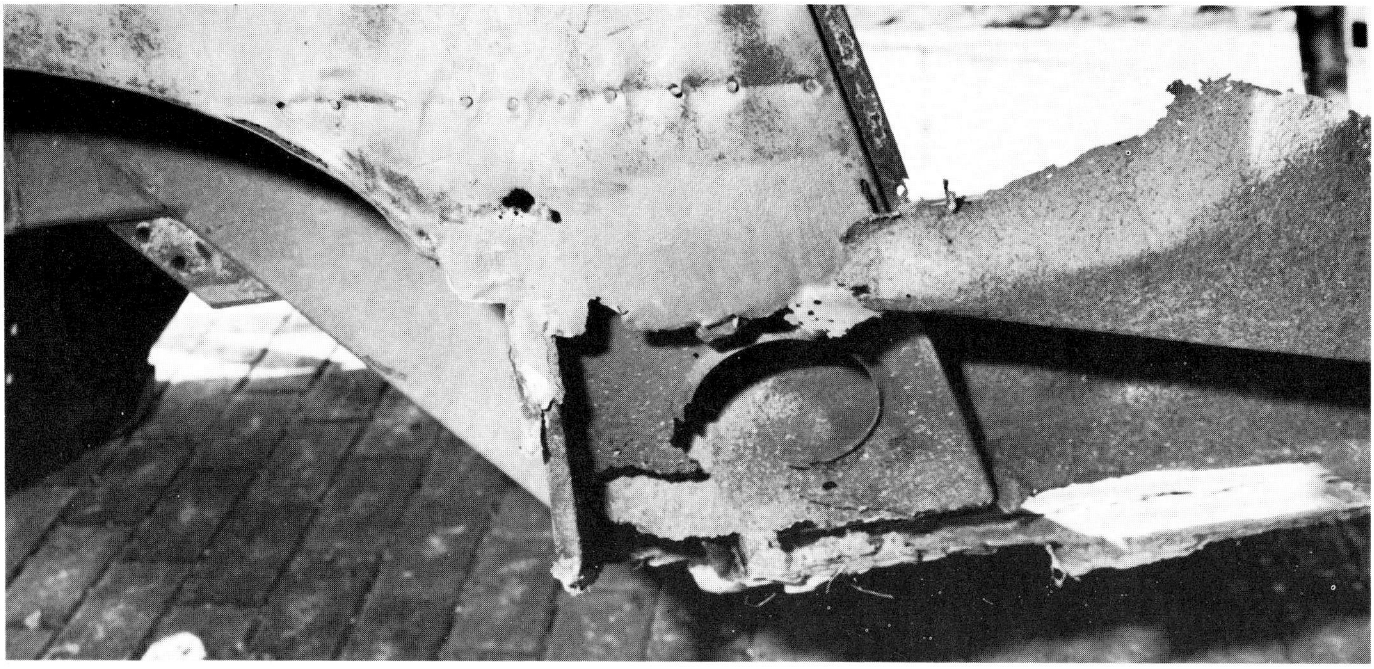

top

Replacing the sills never ends at renewing the outer covers, and you should always be prepared for this kind of horror. In this case the door post (as well as everything else) will have to be rebuilt.

middle right

Rear wheel arches are yet another trouble spot on the E-type, water getting trapped in the double-skinned section and rotting from the inside.

bottom right

Corrosion under the coupé's rear side window.

top left

The sills always rot first and have generally been replaced more than once. Often these kinds of holes have been filled on the outside . . .

bottom left

. . . but by removing the sill trims in the cabin you may find scenes like this: rot caused by condensation inside the sill has eaten the floor-to-sill joint away.

box sections that brace the car on each side to take the rear suspension assembly. The classic rust problem here is around where the radius arms are mounted, corrosion, cracks or amateurish plate welding causing the car to almost literally 'break its back' just below the door posts. In really bad cases the entire rear suspension assembly has been known to come adrift when the car is driven in a spirited fashion over a hump backed-bridge, which is embarrassing and very dangerous. Untold mechanical damage would also be caused, as the propshaft would still be attached to the rear suspension. It doesn't bear thinking about . . . With the rear wheels removed you can check out the arched box members inside the wheel arches that carry the rear suspension mounting points on either side, plus the bump stop mountings (which often appear sound at a quick glance) and the anti-roll bar attachment points.

There's another big trouble spot on the rear wings of all models. On the coupés a water trap where the inner wing meets the outer wing causes rot all around this double-skinned arch and the problems generally continue underneath the bumper. Rot can also appear on the joint between the top of the rear wing and the bodyshell itself, the lead filler used on this joint lifting over the years and eventually allowing water in. It's a similar story on the roadster, although yet more problems are caused by the hood tacking strip, a wooden strip about an inch wide and a quarter of an inch deep which runs along the back of the roadster from one side to the other. As its title

left
This shows the effects of water collecting under the seal that goes round the rear door aperture on the fixed-head coupé.

suggests the hood is tacked on to this strip and it is then covered by a piece of chrome. However, because of the water retention properties of the wooden strip it eventually starts to rot the wing and the surrounding recesses.

Filler, incidentally, is very effective at hiding outer wheel arch rot (and rust on the section under the bumper where the inner and outer skins meet) so make sure there's a nice clean single-thickness rebate all round the arch, anything else indicating body filler. On coupés you may be able to find a patch of rust just underneath the rear side window, too. Further worthwhile checks at the back of the car include the panel above the number plate and the panel behind the plate itself. Inside the boot examine the fuel tank, the spare wheel well around the edges and where the strengtheners are spot welded. From underneath examine the outer corners of the boot floor and the joint between the outer and centre sections. On the coupé, rust can sometimes be found beneath the rubber seal that runs around the rear door aperture.

The doors are a bad spot on all E-types, rot usually starting at the bottom of the outer skins, caused by water getting in through faulty window seals. Look underneath the door, paying particular attention to the folded joint on the outer skin where it's folded round the door frame. You are looking for a clean, straight fold but generally you will find that the joint is covered in glassfibre or has had plates riveted on. The door is hung on a single hinge, which wears particularly badly on the 2-plus-2 model because of its longer doors.

Boot lids and rear luggage doors on roadsters and coupés tend to rot below the

bottom left
Rot underneath the chrome trim at the top of the front screen pillar on a coupé.

right, both pictures
Rotten door bottoms caused by water collecting in the crimped-over joint between the outer skin and inner frame.

'Jaguar E-type' badges and around the lower edges, and although this kind of damage can be repaired by letting in new metal or by leading you are generally better off replacing these panels altogether as they are freely available and not especially expensive.

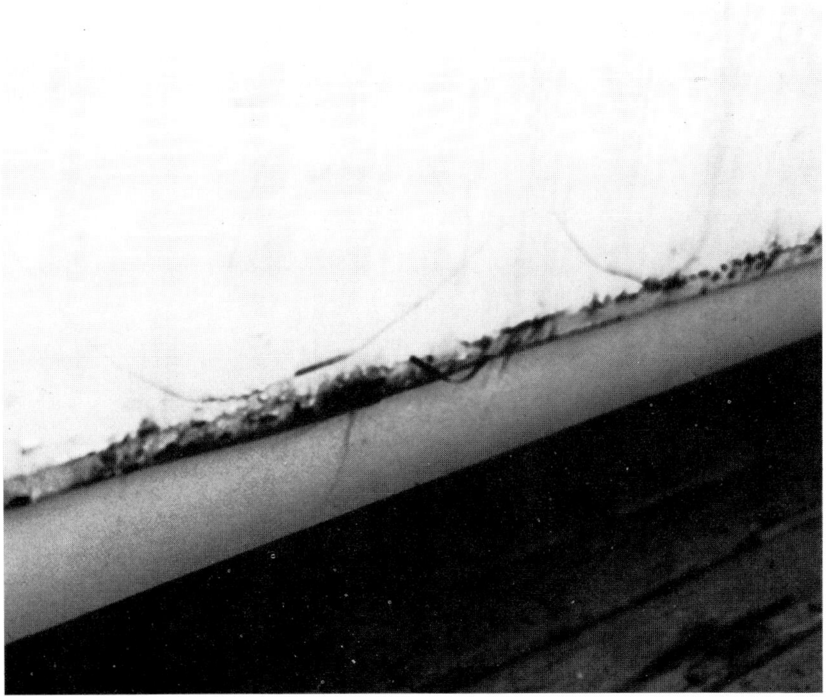

There isn't that much chrome on the E-type to check out, which is useful because most of it isn't of particularly good quality and like most brightwork of this era doesn't replate very well.

Finding a bodily sound E-type for high days and holidays use isn't easy and such cars will not be cheap. The cars to avoid, as always, are the ones that seem superficially acceptable but just need tidying here and there. You may think that you are getting a bargain with a car like this but in reality it is more likely to need a total rebuild and you would have been better off buying a much cheaper 'basket case' restoration project in the first place. As time goes by supplies of restoration projects – especially in two-seater form – will start to dry up, and I doubt if there is any such thing as a roadster E-type that is beyond economical help these days. If you do decide to go for a rebuild car make sure it comes complete, as chasing round after obscure parts can be very irritating and time consuming, especially if you are not altogether sure what they look like.

Interior and hood

Though rather cramped, the E-type's cockpit always looked the part and was nicely detailed. The facia was dominated by a handsome wood-rimmed steering wheel, with three drilled aluminium spokes, supplied by the Coventry Timber Bending Co. Ltd. Beech veneers were employed, hand finished and polished on a lathe. Directly behind the wheel was a big Smiths speedo calibrated to 160mph, with white markings on a black background, and a matching rev counter incorporating a clock. A drop-down centre panel finished in aluminium housed an impressive line-up of four Smiths dials, giving information on amps, fuel, oil pressure and water temperature, with an old fashioned rotary light switch in the middle. Along the bottom was a row of clearly marked black toggle switches controlling the interior lights, panel lights, two-speed fan, map light, two-speed windscreen wipers and electric screen washer. A cigar lighter was placed in the centre of the row, with the key-operated ignition switch to the left and the separate starter button to the right. The fresh air and heater controls were mounted next to the glove box (there were ducts beneath the scuttle at each side and demisting ducts at the base of the screen) with the choke lever in a vertical quadrant on the opposite side next to the rev counter. The horn button was in the centre of the steering wheel boss and the indicator/headlamp flasher lever was mounted on the steering column, which incidentally was adjustable for reach and rake. The centre console, with its housings for a radio and twin speakers, and the gearbox tunnel cover had the same aluminium finish as the central

above

The 3.8 E-type's cabin always looked good, but comfort was not a strong point. Those bucket seats were not too comfortable and had little available adjustment, and the flat floor meant that long legs tended to foul the steering wheel.

right

The useful rear load area of the coupé, the main limitation on space being the sloping roof. The load area was four feet long and covered with Hardura matting. There was a luggage retaining board just behind the rear seats, shown here in its lowered position. The spare wheel and tool roll lived under the removable board on the right.

Q BATTERY
4201 VC

instrument panel. Proper bucket seats were a feature of the 3.8 cars, finished in unquilted leather over foam rubber cushions, and although they looked extremely purposeful many people found their shape uncomfortable.

With the 4.2 came quite a number of interior changes, some of which had first been seen on late model 3.8s. Much bigger, thickly padded seats were introduced, with a facility for altering the rake of the squab a little. The car gained an extra oddments box between the seats but the aluminium finish on the centre panel and gearbox tunnel was dispensed with, the former having the same black finish as the rest of the dash and the latter a vinyl covering to match the colour of the seats. The hinges on the rear door of the closed car were covered to prevent damaging the luggage, there was a one-piece luggage mat and the wheel arch humps were trimmed in vinyl instead of cloth. Door arm rests were another new feature.

The 2-plus-2 car introduced a couple of years later gained a parcel shelf, hazard warning lights, anti-burst locks, a lid for the glove compartment and, most important of all, variable direction outlet nozzles for the heating and ventilation system. All these features, bar the parcel shelf, were also introduced on the standard-wheelbase Series 2 cars in 1968, along with XJ6-type rocker switches, a separate clock, recessed heating and choke controls and a snap-off rear view mirror. The seats were redesigned, and recessed door handles and rounded window winder knobs were introduced, all in the interests of safety.

By the standards of 1961, the E-type's hood was generally satisfactory. Made in mohair in Jaguar's own trim shop, they were tailored for each car and looked extremely neat. The rear window was fairly big and the hood could be raised or lowered while sitting in the car – it was simply a matter of securing or undoing three over-centre toggle clamps. The hood was reasonably watertight and looked neat when stowed in its envelope. A very nicely proportioned glassfibre hardtop was available from the factory, and a number of viable alternatives followed from other sources. The factory item cost around £76.

right

A Series 1 4.2 cockpit, showing the much more civilized seats, the vinyl trim on the centre console, and the floor footwells introduced a few months into the production of the 3.8.

above

The Series 1 4.2 centre panel was finished in black, but was otherwise identical to the 3.8.

left

Series 1 instruments framed by the lovely wood-rimmed wheel. The rev counter is common to all Jaguars of the period but the speedo was a 160mph item unique to the E-type. The slide control on the left is for the choke.

above

Main changes to the Series 2 facia were new rocker switches, recessed choke and heater controls and a lid for the glove box. The separate starter button had gone and the clock moved from its position in the rev counter (which was now electric) to the centre panel.

top right

Usable if not generous rear compartment of a 2-plus-2, with room for two small children or an adult seated sideways.

left

Rear compartment of a 2-plus-2 with the seats folded, giving 4ft 3½in of load space.

bottom right

A typically rough looking E-type cabin. All parts are available but they often don't fit correctly.

Most of the interior is quite easily replaceable. Many people simply buy complete re-trim kits that they can fit themselves, usually consisting of hide seat covers, a tunnel and console kit, carpets, Hardura mats for the cabin and boot, vinyl sill trim, underfelt and insulation material, door trim panels and a vinyl covered steel trim set. These kits are certainly a good idea but often the bits don't fit well because every car is slightly different, so a more expensive alternative is to have your car refurbished inside by a trimmer, who can tailor everything to the correct size. Most of the jobs aren't that hard: in theory (and if the bolts that hold it were free) you could retrim a seat and have it back inside the car in an hour or so. There are few items you cannot get for the E-type's interior, and of course certain switches and dials are common to Jaguar saloon models, although the 160mph speedo is only fitted to the E-type. Moto-Lita make fine replicas of the E-type's steering wheel.

0 DFD

left
The works hardtop on a very early 3.8.

The roadster's hood is fixed to a wooden tacking strip at the back which rots with age, the tacks then pulling out of the strip, causing the hood to lose its tension when pulled up. Fitting a reproduction hood that is the correct shape is no problem but nine times out of ten they don't fit properly. Often you end up with the door catching the hood, which means cutting and trimming the hood and then sewing it all back up again.

above
A 2-plus-2 Series 2 coupé awaiting restoration. A car this rough can be bought relatively cheaply because it makes no secret of its condition, whereas you can pay a lot more for an apparently smarter car which is actually just as bad.

Restoration

Rebuilding the bodywork of a Jaguar E-type is not at all straightforward. You would need to be very skilful and knowledgeable to put a badly rusted car to rights, although having said that a few novices have tackled these cars with a degree of success. In any event someone thinking of restoring an E-type needs to be very confident in his skills, have plenty of time, the right equipment and lots and lots of money. We will discuss the problems to be faced in more detail later.

Mechanically the prospects are much brighter. Though not a simple unit the XK engine has no tricks up its sleeve and can quite easily be rebuilt by a competent DIY man with the right tools, a proper workshop manual and, if possible, someone nearby with knowledge of the engine to appeal to for help. Much the same goes for the suspension, steering and braking systems.

Spares supply is no problem. All engine parts are available, most trim items can be bought off the shelf and the list of remanufactured body parts is increasing by the month. Jaguar still supply most of the bonnets (and many other parts) but as these panels are pressed in batches Jaguar do not produce them until quite a number of orders have built up, so you may have to wait a while for a factory bonnet. As with all E-type parts,

right
Excellent welding skills will be required if you are to take on the restoration of an E-type's body.

left
As well as the standard Jaguar hardtop, which was the most attractive, numerous private firms offered alternatives, such as this rather square looking affair from Lenham.

left

Replacement parts should not be a problem, as this picture of Martin Robey's stores suggests.

right

If you have a rotten E-type but don't have the skills or time to restore it, then you can now have a virtually new bodyshell built around your car. These shots were taken at Martin E Robey's premises in Warwickshire, where you can have your car rebuilt to one of three stages according to how much you can afford. Note the jig underneath the shell, which is essential if the body of the car is not to distort when the rusty parts are cut out.

what isn't available right away will be before too long, and if you can't get the part you want from a specialist it's always worth checking out your local Jaguar dealer, who may still have the part you want listed on his computer.

Thankfully most of the 'cock-up' merchants in the E-type restoration world have fallen by the wayside now, although there's a new generation of restoration firms coming up all the time who are more interested in making money than doing a good job. Of course there's always a good case for having a well-established restorer tackle the bodywork on your E-type, and for some years now Martin E Robey in the Midlands has been offering 'system' rebuilds using only the front bulkhead from your rotted-out car. System 1 is a bodyshell without doors, bonnet or boot lid, System 2 is a shell with doors and a boot lid, and the most expensive System 3 rebuild is a complete shell with the doors, boot lid and bonnet.

left

A complete new monocoque being built up.

top right

The only section of the original car that is retained is the front bulkhead, the rest being completely new.

bottom right

Fewer coupés than roadsters are being rebuilt from scratch in the Robey fashion at the moment because they are not as valuable and rebuild costs cannot always be recouped.

Martin Robey is just about to introduce a system rebuild, priced below the basic System 1 shell, which includes all the floors, chassis sections and frame mounting points but doesn't have any of the outer body panels fitted. This is a good way of getting all the really hard structural aspects of a body restoration out of the way, leaving the home restorer to fit the outer panels himself. All the system rebuild cars are jig built and lead loaded ready for the paint shop, and the prices include whatever it costs to restore your original bulkhead too. Most of the cars that have been rebuilt in this way have been roadsters, as the coupés are more expensive to do and are not as valuable at the end of the day. Purists may look down their noses slightly at cars rebuilt this way as they are effectively brand new E-type shells, but if you have the kind of money required then one of Robey's cars seems like an excellent way of avoiding the considerable hassle of restoring your E-type's bodywork. Apparently many enthusiasts agree, as there is a 12 to 15 month waiting list for the System 3 shell.

But if you regard bodywork restoration as 'fun', and really do want to carry out as much of the work yourself as possible, what sort of problems are you likely to come up against? Panel fit is a very important point to consider, because the E-type was hand-assembled to a certain extent, and although you can get panels to hang on the car correctly they very often don't fit properly in relation to other panels, each car being ever so slightly different. The bonnet is a classic example: usually the offside front wing is too long – ovelapping the bulkhead – and too deep – overlapping the sill. Grinding off the excess length is fairly straightforward but the part that overlaps the sill has a wired and rolled edge, which means prising the metal away where it's lipped over the wire, pulling the wire out (the wire is there to give a nice round edge, incidentally) cutting off as much metal as you think is necessary and then hammering the edge back over the wire. Most amateurs attempting this kind of job would struggle (leaving their hammer marks, etc.) because it really takes 20 years of experience to do these sorts of jobs properly.

If you want absolute originality then lead is the only filler to use on joints and when building up contours on the car, as this was what Jaguar originally used on the E-type. However, it should be said that filler technology has come a long way in recent years and filler is generally much easier for the home restorer to use. If possible, try to acquire both gas and Mig welding equipment. Gas is flexible, being useful for cutting and for freeing bolts, etc., as well as welding, but the Mig equipment is easier to learn to use and better for welding up big panels as distortion is much more localized. If you do have to tie yourself down to one or the other, however, gas is probably the plant to go for.

above and left

Fitting the bonnet is a very skilled job because it is extremely difficult to get the shut lines correct. Shims have to be used at the fitting stage to get the lines absolutely right, and are fitted between the hinge and bonnet at the front.

Series 3 roadster and coupé keeping company.

The frontal aspect of the Series 3 was less harmonious than that of the Series 1 cars.

Series 3 roadster, the most sought-after E-type.

300 MP

Cockpit of the Series 3 roadster.

This side-by-side shot of Series 3 and 3.8 roadsters brings home the differences in appearance between the two.

For the sake of originality, lead is the only type of filler to use, as Jaguar used large quantities to build up contours in the bodywork.

The E-type monocoque, particularly in roadster form, distorts easily when important structural pieces are removed, so it's vital to get some reference points by taking measurements before you start to strip the car. The car also has to be firmly supported on the chassis rails – four axle stands would do but a proper jig is obviously ideal, though few people have this kind of equipment at home. A car with a distorted bodyshell can end up crab-tracked and will never behave properly on the road.

Most E-type bonnets will have rusted to some extent and as I have mentioned before it's generally better to replace the whole bonnet than mess about trying to repair the original item. They are always more rusty than they look and parts to repair them are pretty expensive; by the time you have finished buying, say, two wings, a bonnet mounting panel and other bits and pieces the bill could have come to more than half of what a complete factory bonnet would have cost. Most of the parts are difficult to fit, too: the inner diaphragms for instance have to be stuck to the bonnet centre panel with metal to metal adhesive to avoid welding distortion, but getting the two to stick is very often a problem.

Replacing the sills on an E-type is a bigger operation than it sounds. You have to melt all the old lead out of the sill joints at the bottom of the rear wing and the bulkhead after grinding the outer cover off, and then see how far the rot has gone. It has almost always progressed a lot further than you at first thought, and you will often end up replacing the rear wing – or at best fitting a repair section for the bottom of the wing and above the sill plus a similar piece for the scuttle area at the front. Nine times out of ten, though, outer sill problems warn that the whole monocoque has rotted, and you will be lucky if major restoration work is not required.

Floor sections are surprisingly easy to fit. Simply grind away the spot welds, clean all the edges and then just drop the footwell in and weld it up. If that's all that's wrong underneath, then a couple of footwells can transform the look of the car's floorpan.

A new door structure being finished.

The radius arm mounting points are a problem area, being fully exposed to the elements, and like the sills rust here is rarely localized. Rust starts where the floor goes up towards the rear suspension at the rear of the radius arm mounting point, and also between the mounting point and the sill edges. You can buy a new mounting point section to repair this area or a rear floor section complete.

There's a good water trap around the bump stop areas and inner rear wings. Replacing the inner and outer rear wings tends to be more difficult on the coupé models because of the way the two sections are joined inside above the wheel, which makes them difficult to get at. They need to be well sealed, too, if future corrosion is to be avoided. The job is more straightforward on the roadster as it has no inner arch.

If a door frame is rotten you will have to replace the whole thing but if you are lucky only the skins will be rusty and replacing them is fairly easy. All you have to do is strip the door down to its bare state and remove the skin by grinding away the edges all the way round until it comes off. You don't even need any welding gear to put the new skin on as it is simply crimped onto the frame. However, you will probably find that the gaps are all wrong when you offer the door up, in which case you may have to grind it away slightly at the front edge and possibly add a line of Mig weld on the back edge, then lead it to get the right shape. It's difficult at the best of times to get doors to fit but worn hinges will make the problem even worse.

The front subframe tubing can be repaired but it makes more sense to buy a new subframe assembly. The tubes rot from the inside out and although you may have repaired the obvious sections there's often another area of rot on the verge of breaking out that you don't know about.

Despite appearances the XK unit is very much a 'common sense' engine and anyone with a workshop manual, the right tools and some mechanical knowlege should be able to rebuild it with few real problems. It's rather a pleasant engine to work on in fact, the main snag for the home mechanic being its sheer weight and bulk. The official Jaguar workshop manual goes into all the ins and outs of rebuilding one of these units but a number of points need to be stressed. Getting the engine

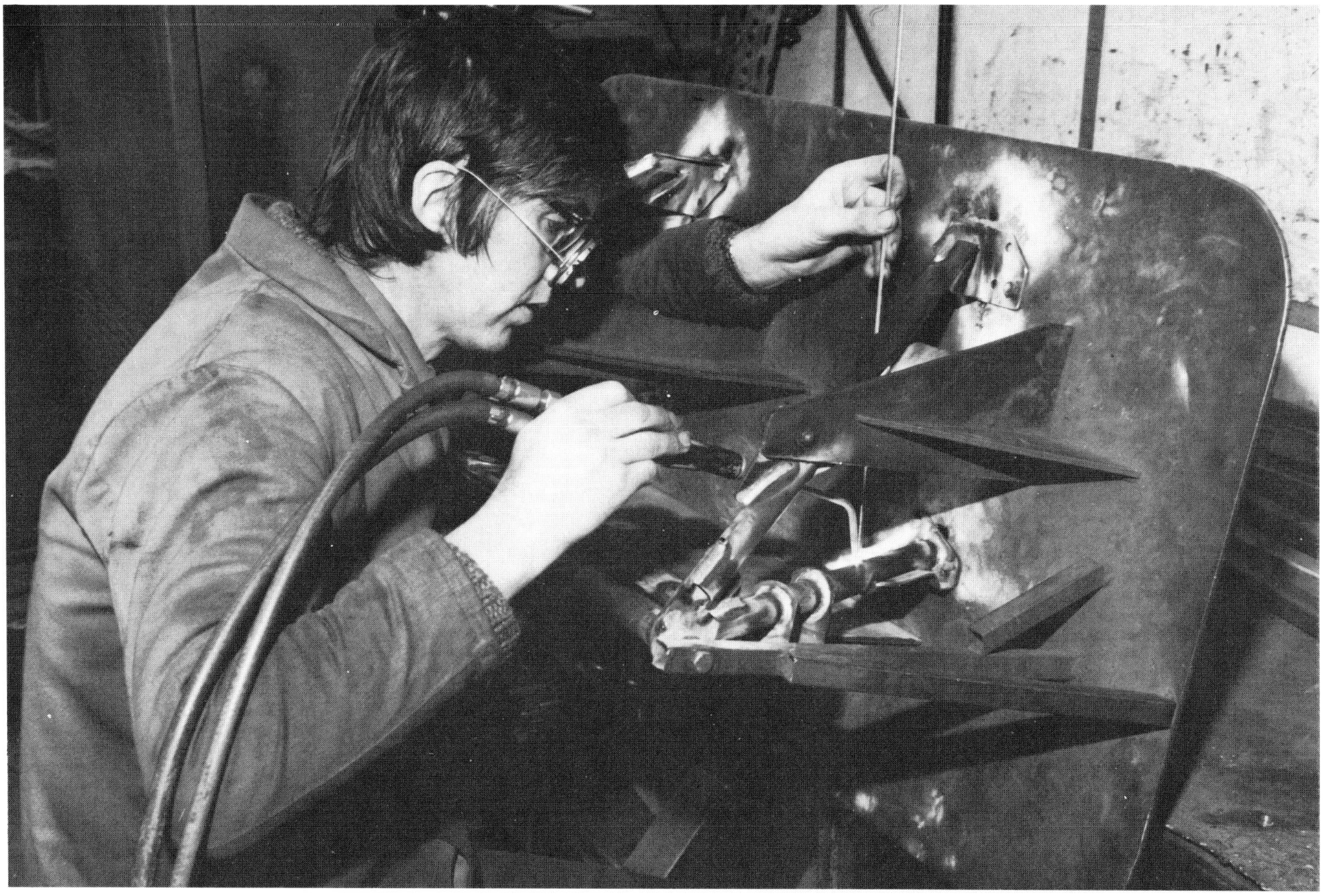

Complete new subframes are available for the E-type. Here a new one is being built up on a jig.

out of the car is not at all simple, although the job is made slightly easier by the fact that the whole front end can be removed (don't forget to store the bonnet in a safe place where it can't get damaged). The lifting straps on most cars are on the cylinder head and, as on almost all XK-engined Jaguars, you can't remove the engine without taking the gearbox out too. You will need a hoist that is capable of lifting 8cwt and when lifting the unit you have to be careful that it does not jam on the torsion bar mounting. There isn't much clearance between the water pump and the 'picture frame' at the front either. It would take a DIY man a good two days to get the engine out of an E-type.

As far as dismantling the engine goes, it's well worth cleaning it off with Gunk or the like before you split it from the gearbox. Instead of buying new parts for the engine as you go along the best idea would probably be to buy a rebuild kit from one of the specialists, which includes all the little nuts, bolts, gaskets and seals as well as the major items like pistons and bearings. Because five star fuel is no longer available you would be well advised to fit 8:1 compression ratio pistons. When rebuilding the unit a common mistake is not sealing the oil feed pipes properly inside the pump, so that the pump starts pulling up air as well as oil, causing a loss of oil pressure. If you have never done an XK cylinder head before, be warned that it's easy to bend valves when you are setting the tappets.

Both Moss and synchromesh Jaguar gearboxes are very strong and rarely require rebuilding, though when they do they are fairly straightforward and can be done at home – everything inside is big and strong and it's just a case of following a logical sequence of steps and keeping everything clean. Parts can be difficult, but the situation is getting better.

There's little that can be said about the front suspension except that it's simple to dismantle and everything is easy to recondition, but on the rather exposed steering system bolts are often seized up and some of them are hard to get at. The Metalastic bushes usually need replacing – worn ones cause the rack to move about when the wheel is turned, thus giving a vague feeling to the steering – and although it's possible to recondition your old rack it's always better to buy a relatively inexpensive new one as rebuilding them can be awkward.

The rear suspension subframe is as much of a rebuild proposition for the DIY man as the engine is. It's a complicated, heavy unit and getting it off the car is at least a two-man job. It's attached to the car via four Metalastic mountings bolted to the chassis and where the radius arm mounting points are attached, the problem here being that the mountings seize to the cups; there is a special tool available for parting them or you can do it with an air chisel. You usually find wear in the hub bearings, inner and outer fulcrum bearings and the universal joints but all these can be rectified without removing the frame from the car. Any work on the differential unit, however, means that the subframe has to come out because the bolts that hold the unit in are right at the top of the subframe in the centre. It's well worth overhauling the subframe unit completely once it is out to save yourself trouble later.

The Dunlop brakes fitted to Series 1 cars give the most trouble. If you find that the bolt-on piston assemblies have seized up they are almost certain to be corroded and pitted inside, and it's not worth trying to rebuild them. The Girling units on Series 2s aren't such a problem and can be rebuilt if need be. The front brakes are easy to get at on all models but the rear calipers are almost inaccessible without the suspension subframe being taken out, though taking the halfshafts out allows the discs to move to a certain extent. New servos are expensive and sometimes difficult to get hold of, but kits are available to rebuild them.

Running and maintenance

Fifteen or twenty years ago, when the E-type was the cheapest really fast car you could buy new or secondhand, it tended to attract a certain type of owner, one who could just about stretch to the asking price but begrudged forking out for regular maintenance and certainly wasn't going to get his hands dirty himself – it was a case of liking the image and 'bird pulling' appeal of the car but not wanting any of the responsibility. No wonder so many unrestored E-types are in such poor mechanical shape today. Of course the six-cylinder E-types actually rate as very practical machines to run and maintain considering their performance and complexity; certainly there's no other genuine supercar capable of close on 150mph that can be tackled by a competent DIY man, and few are as docile to drive around town. The number of people who really do use their E-types regularly goes down every year as the cars become more valuable, but the E-type could quite easily be pressed into service as day-to-day transport on today's roads with no real problems. Fuel consumption is not excessive (18mpg under mixed conditions is a usual figure), there's plenty of luggage space in the fixed-head model, and, best of all, reliability is generally good because all the mechanical bits are very well proven.

Naturally, some versions are more practical than others. At one extreme the 3.8, with its awkward gearbox, questionable brakes and uncomfortable bucket seats, would not be a particularly practical everyday machine, but a 2-plus-2 (in Series 2 form especially) would be very nearly as usable as an XJ6 saloon, with good brakes, a nice gear change and plenty of room for small children in the back seats. With all models, parking in a confined space presents a problem as the front three feet of the bonnet are impossible for the average sized driver to see, while drivers of vans or lorries sometimes don't see the low-slung E-type at all when they park, so it usually pays to park your E well away from other vehicles if possible.

The majority of maintenance jobs on the E-type are quite straightforward. Regular lubrication of the car in various places is very important, and apart from oil and filter changes every 3000 miles, topping up the carburettor piston dampers, etc., there are greasing points on the chassis for the steering rack and pinion, tie rods, wheel swivels, front and rear wheel bearings, and outer and inner pivot bearings on the rear suspension.

Maintaining the top end of the engine may present one or two problems for someone more used to a single-cam pushrod engined sports car like an MGB. On the XK engine you adjust tappet clearances not by turning a screw but by means of special shims that are available from Jaguar dealers in various thicknesses. After removing the cam covers you have to check the clearance between the back of each cam and its tappet and then note them down, the correct clearances for the early E-types being .004″ for inlet and .006″ for exhaust valves. The shims, or adjusting pads, are lettered A to Z on the surface, each letter signifying an increase in size of .001″. If the clearances do need correcting you have to remove the camshafts, tappets and shims (and then measure the thickness of each shim with a micrometer if the letter on the surface indicating the size is no longer visible). If you find that the clearance on, say, No 1 valve is .010″ when it should be .006″ you then use a shim that is .004″ thicker than the one you remove. It's important to remember to do one camshaft at a time when setting the tappets and to release the other camshaft to close the valves – otherwise you will end up with a bent valve or two. A camshaft setting tool (which came in the tool kit of the E-type when new) is pretty essential, this half-moon shaped plate with a cut-out in the top ensuring that the cams are in the right position when the engine is at TDC. Another useful tool is a timing chain adjuster, which is used for tensioning the top timing chain when it becomes noisy. The adjuster plate, which can be found beneath the breather housing, has in simple terms to be rotated anti-clockwise by the adjuster until the chain is tensioned but not dead tight.

Replacing the clutch on an E-type is an engine-out job that will take two experienced men a couple of days to complete if everything goes well. In the late sixties and early seventies when the E-type was not thought of as a classic, many backstreet garages did a roaring trade in removing the gearbox from inside the car by hacking the transmission tunnel away . . .

Servicing the rear suspension could give the amateur problems but, with a bit of patience and thought, working on this unit is not by any means beyond the scope of the home mechanic. Removing the four springs and dampers, for instance, is fairly straightforward (as long as the mounting bolts and shafts have not seized) although the top mounting is a bit difficult to get at. The spring and damper come off as one unit which then has to be split on the bench using a very strong set of spring compressors – remember that compressed coil springs can be killers. It's well worth replacing the four Metalastic bushes on the rear suspension every few years even though this is a time-consuming job which involves removal of the rear suspension unit. If you do have to take the rear subframe out, that is the time to check the propshaft universal joints as you can't get the propshaft off without removing this unit or the engine.

Servicing the front brakes is no problem but the rear units are quite awkward to get at because of their inboard position. Long wheelbase cars have an inspection panel under the rear seat that can be removed so you can check the pads for wear and take them out from the top if necessary. In days gone by owners would cut holes in the floors of their two-seater E-types for the same reason, though that's not really on today no matter how practical it may seem. You can just about get the rear calipers off without removing the subframe (though the official workshop manual says otherwise) but not the discs. The handbrake on later cars is supposed to be self adjusting but it rarely works properly – you have to disconnect the cable and adjust it for the right amount of movement on the lever in the cabin. If the handbrake calipers have seized up or the pads have worn then no amount of adjustment will get the handbrake to work efficiently. Although it is possible to change the handbrake pads with the subframe *in situ* it's always better in the long run – as with most brake jobs – to drop the subframe and do everything properly.

On a more general note, the 185/15 tyres fitted to the E-type can now be a little difficult to get hold of, and though some people fit oversize tyres these don't really do a lot for the roadholding or handling and tend to foul the bump stops. When jacking up the E-type, incidentally, always lift the car under the central jacking socket below the sill (there are two on the 2-plus-2) or under the lower wishbone at the front. Never use the subframe tubes, which are easily damaged.

Keeping rust at bay is obviously important so give all box sections regular doses of waxoyl and pay particular attention to the bonnet. Underseal is not worth bothering with as it tends to trap water and salt in cracks as it dries out and quickens the rusting process. If you have a rusty bonnet on your E-type and can't afford a new one right away, don't dismiss the idea of fitting a temporary glassfibre replacement, as they are of extremely high quality these days and will not rust. Of course they devalue the car considerably and don't have the correct finish on the underside, but having one of these fitted has to be better than driving around with a steel bonnet that is crumbling before your eyes.

Cost guidelines

It may seem hard to believe now but only a dozen years ago you could pick up a decent early E-type for well under £1000. As a small boy the author can well remember watching in horror as his father turned down the chance of a flat floor coupé for only £800! Since then things have obviously changed a great deal; the E-type is one of the most sought-after mass-produced classics there is and as nostalgia for the sixties grows prices can only get higher. Already the best cars are realizing sums most people wouldn't have dreamed of only five years ago, although it has to be said that compared with a lot of exclusive Italian exotica the good old E-type still rates as a lot of car for the money.

Roadsters, especially in 3.8 form, bring the most money and really top condition machines are now well into the five figure bracket, with the early flat floor cars commanding a slight premium because of their rarity. A merely good 3.8 drophead still breaks the five figure barrier with ease and even basket cases – needing a complete rebuild – can cost as much as a good 2-plus-2! 4.2 roadsters come just a little cheaper but are very much in the same price range and, perhaps surprisingly, there's virtually no difference between Series 1 and 2 values: some want the speed and purer looks of the Series 1, while others prefer the greater practicality of the later car. Two-seater fixed-head cars can generally be bought for just over a third of the price of a roadster depending on condition, although the difference in price between 3.8 and 4.2 cars is perhaps not quite so great. Again, the best cars are well into the ten thousand-plus bracket. The 2-plus-2 six cylinder cars have always been the poor relations of the E-type family, basically because they don't look as nice or go quite as well as the standard wheelbase models, though they are cheaper and much more practical. However, like the rest of the range the 2-plus-2's prices have been going up and you can now get a nice example for perhaps £1000 to £1500 less than an equivalent two-seater coupé. If anything a Series 2 model may fetch just a little more than the earlier car, possibly because buyers tend to prefer its less upright looking windscreen. The nearest thing to an E-type 'bargain' you can get these days is a 2-plus-2 automatic.

The international motoring press admiring the 3.8 E-type fixed-head at Geneva in 1961; no British car had caused such a sensation since the XK120 of 1948. This car, registered 9600 HP, was timed at 150mph by Autocar, *although some years later it was found to have a blueprinted engine, an aluminium rear door and perspex side windows.*

This is how 9600 HP has ended up. It is now in the hands of Jaguar historian Philip Porter, who plans to restore the car.

True, it's easily the least desirable variant but it is worth thinking about if you can't quite afford a manual car and it certainly shouldn't be written off out of hand. Usually you can pick up a decent auto for perhaps £750 to £1000 less than a manual 2-plus-2 in good order. If you picked up a car at the right price then it might be worthwhile doing a gearbox transplant if you really must have a manual 'box.

In a nutshell

Back in 1961 it seemed that everybody wanted to own a Jaguar E-type and even now few, if any, high performance glamour cars hold the same fascination for such a large number of enthusiasts. They still look fantastic and perform superbly. Although the car's pretty expensive to buy, prices are not yet in the realms of fantasy – indeed some of the less exalted versions can be bought for less than the price of a good medium-sized 1.6 litre saloon. Make no mistake, the six-cylinder Series 1 and 2 E-types have one hell of a lot going for them in the classic desirability stakes.

The main problem facing the E-type buyer is that there's such a large amount of scope for tarting up these cars; rusty bonnets, wheel arches and sills can all be disguised very easily with filler while a quick blow over and a new set of carpets can make the roughest car look like a million dollars. As with most classics, there's very little middle ground between really sound cars and restoration project basket cases, and few seemingly moderately priced, driveable, tidy looking cars will not be rusty under the skin. Often it's more sensible to buy a car for restoration relatively cheaply than blow quite a few thousand pounds on an E with an MOT that 'just needs tidying up'; don't kid yourself into thinking that your problems will end with a new set of sills because before you know where you are you will be into a total restoration. And, of course, few cars are so complex or mind blowingly expensive to restore as an E-type: they rot very comprehensively, putting the body back to rights is no job for an inexperienced restorer, as I have explained, and paying somebody else to do it will cost a frightening amount because of the number of skilled man hours that will be needed. All the mechanical bits, especially the engine and rear suspension, are also very expensive to have rebuilt, though they are more of a DIY proposition than the bodywork. It's all too easy to be swayed into buying almost any E-type because of the superb looks and performance, so enter the business of buying one of these cars with your eyes wide open; find out all the pitfalls (read this book through again), if you want a car you can run be suspicious of anything that seems cheap, and put the condition of the bodywork above all other considerations.

SPECIFICATIONS

	E-type 3.8 roadster and coupé	E-type 4.2 Series 1 roadster and coupé
Engine	In-line six	In-line six
Construction	Cast-iron block, alloy head	Cast-iron block, alloy head
Main bearings	Seven	Seven
Bore/Stroke	87×106mm	92.07×106mm
Capacity	3781cc	4235cc
Valves	Twin OHC	Twin OHC
Compression ratio	9:1 (8:1 optional)	9:1 (8:1 optional)
Fuel system	Three 2in SU HD8 carburettors	Three 2in SU HD8 carburettors
Power	265bhp (gross) at 5500rpm	265bhp (gross) at 5400rpm
Torque	260lb ft at 4000rpm	283lb ft at 4000rpm
Transmission	Four-speed manual	Four-speed manual
Top gear	24.8mph at 1000rpm in top	24.4mph at 1000rpm in top
Final drive	3.31:1 (optional 2.93, 3.27, 3.07, 3.54, 3.77, 4.09)	3.07 (optional 2.93, 3.27, 3.31, 3.54, 3.77,4.09)
Brakes	Dunlop discs all round, 11in front, 10in rear	Dunlop discs all round, 11in front, 10in rear
Suspension front	Ind. by wishbones and torsion bars, with Girling telescopic dampers	Ind. by wishbones and torsion bars, with Girling telescopic dampers
Suspension rear	Ind. by lower wishbones with radius arms and twin coil springs, with Girling telescopic dampers. Upper location by halfshafts	Ind. by lower wishbones with radius arms and twin coil springs, with Girling telescopic dampers. Upper location by halfshafts
Steering	Rack and pinion	Rack and pinion
Wheels/tyres	Centre-lock wire wheels, 5in rims. 6.40-15in tyres	Centre-lock wire wheels. 5in rims. 6.40-15in tyres
Body	All-steel body, monocoque up to front bulkhead with space subframe at front. 2-door roadster or 3-door coupé	All-steel body, monocoque up to front bulkhead with space subframe at front. 2-door roadster or 3-door coupé

DIMENSIONS

Length	14ft 7¼in	14ft 7¼in
Width	5ft 5¼in	5ft 5¼in
Height	3ft 11in (roadster) 4ft (coupé)	3ft 11in (roadster) 4ft (coupé)
Wheelbase	8ft	8ft
Unladen weight	24cwt (roadster) 24½cwt (coupé)	24½cwt (roadster) 25cwt (coupé)

SPECIFICATIONS	E-type 4.2 Series 1 2-plus-2	E-type 4.2 Series 2 roadster and coupé
Engine	In-line six	In-line six
Construction	Cast-iron block, alloy head	Cast-iron block, alloy head
Main bearings	Seven	Seven
Bore/Stroke	92.07×106mm	92.07×106mm
Capacity	4235cc	4235cc
Valves	Twin OHC	Twin OHC
Compression ratio	9:1 (8:1 optional)	9:1 (8:1 optional)
Fuel system	Three 2in SU HD8 carburettors	Three 2in SU HD8 carburettors
Power	265bhp (gross) at 5400rpm	265bhp (gross) at 5400rpm 171bhp(DIN) at 4500rpm (emission engine)
Torque	283lb ft at 4000rpm	283lb ft at 4000rpm 230lb ft at 2500rpm (emission engine)
Transmission	Four-speed manual or Borg-Warner Model 8 three-speed automatic	Four-speed manual
Top gear	24.7mph per 1000rpm (manual) 26.4mph per 1000rpm (automatic)	24.7mph per 1000rpm (manual)
Final drive	3.07:1 (optional 2.93, 3.27, 3.31, 3.43, 3.77, 4.09)	3.07:1 (optional 2.93, 3.27, 3.31, 3.54,3.77,4.09)
Brakes	Dunlop discs all round, 11in front, 10in rear	Girling discs all round, 11in front, 10in rear
Suspension, front	Ind. by wishbones and torsion bars, with Girling telescopic dampers	Ind. by wishbones and torsion bars, with Girling telescopic dampers
Suspension, rear	Ind. by lower wishbones with radius arms and twin coils springs, with Girling telescopic dampers. Upper location by halfshafts	Ind. by lower wishbones with radius arms and twin coil springs, with Girling telescopic dampers. Upper location by halfshafts
Steering	Rack and pinion	Rack and pinion, optional power assistance
Wheels/tyres	Centre-lock wire wheels, 5in rims. 185-15in tyres	Centre-lock wire or or bolt-on pressed steel wheels, 5in rims. 185-15in tyres
Body	All-steel body, monocoque up to front bulkhead with space subframe at front. 3-door coupé style only	All-steel body, monocoque up to front bulkhead with space subframe at front. 2-door roadster or 3-door coupé
DIMENSIONS		
Length	15ft 6in	14ft 7¼in
Width	5ft 6in	5ft 5¼
Height	4ft 2½in	3ft 11in (roadster) 4ft(coupé)
Wheelbase	8ft 9in	8ft
Unladen weight	27½cwt	25cwt (roadster) 25½cwt(coupé)

SPECIFICATIONS E-type 4.2 Series 2 2-plus-2

Engine	In-line six
Construction	Cast-iron block, alloy head
Main bearings	Seven
Bore/Stroke	92.07 × 106mm
Capacity	4235cc
Valves	Twin OHC
Compression ratio	9:1 (8:1 optional)
Fuel system	Three 2in SU HD8 carburettors
Power	265bhp(gross) at 5400rpm 171bhp(DIN) at 4500rpm (emission engine)
Torque	283lb ft at 4000rpm 230lb ft at 2500rpm (emission engine)
Transmission	Four-speed manual or Borg-Warner Model 8 three-speed automatic
Top gear	24.7mph per 1000rpm (manual) 26.4mph per 1000rpm(automatic)
Final drive	3.07:1 (optional 2.93, 3.27, 3.31, 3.54, 3.77, 4.09)
Brakes	Girling discs all round, 11in front, 10in rear
Suspension, front	Ind. by wishbones and torsion bars, with Girling telescopic dampers
Suspension, rear	Ind. by lower wishbones with radius arms and twin coil springs, with Girling telescopic dampers. Upper location by halfshafts
Steering	Rack and pinion, optional power assistance
Wheels/tyres	Centre-lock wire or bolt-on pressed steel wheels, 5in. rims. 185-15in tyres
Body	All-steel body, monocoque up to front bulkhead with space subframe at front. 3-door coupé style only

DIMENSIONS

Length	15ft 6in
Width	5ft 6¼in
Height	4ft 2½in
Wheelbase	8ft 9in
Unladen weight	28¾cwt

E-type 5.3 V12

The Series 3 V12 E-type, introduced in 1971. The roadster had the 2-plus-2 wheelbase, though with only two seats. Note the new ventilation grille in this works hardtop-equipped car. An elegant machine, but surely not as beautiful as its predecessors.

By the beginning of the seventies the once muscular E-type had become a shadow of its former self in flabby Series 2 form, and Jaguar were understandably keen to restore some of its lost performance and reputation. The one really effective way of doing this was with a brand new, more powerful engine, and as far as the Browns Lane engineers were concerned the only configuration worth considering was a 60 degree V12; smoother than any in-line six or V8, such an engine would enable Jaguar to challenge the prestige of Ferrari and Lamborghini and at the same time drag the decade-old E-type's performance back into the supercar league. They didn't build the V12 just for the E-type, of course, as the new engine was always destined to power the XJ saloon – using it in the E was simply a good way of sorting out any teething troubles in a fairly low volume model before the commercially more important XJ12 appeared in 1972.

Introduced in April 1971, the new V12 car was known as the 5.3 Series 3, a swansong E-type that was faster, more civilized but sadly less of a true driver's car than any that had gone before it. Today this 'soft' E-type, which was never as well liked in its day as the previous models ('a magnificent engine in an outclassed body' was how *Road and Track* described it) is the most valuable of the lot, and when you add up its many likeable and desirable qualities maybe that isn't so surprising.

Closely related to an abortive four cam hemi-head racing V12 of the early sixties which proved too bulky and inflexible for use in a road car, the production engine of 1971 was a technical masterpiece, generally recognized (even by some Mercedes Benz engineers!) as the finest power unit in quantity production. Designers Bill Heynes, Claude Baily, Harry Mundy and Walter Hassan created the V12 with absolute docility and ease of production in

left

There were numerous changes at the front end, most noticeably a bigger front air intake with a chrome 'bird cage' grille and an air scoop underneath to get more air to the engine. The flared arches are particularly evident in this shot.

below

Rear end of the V12 coupé, now only available in 2-plus-2 form. Apart from the beefy looking four-tailpipe exhaust, through-flow ventilation grille on the door, V12 badge and rubber overrider inserts, the car looked much the same from the back as the Series 2.

mind, which explains the relatively simple 'flat' cylinder head with in-line valves (recessed piston crowns formed the combustion chambers) and a single overhead camshaft for each bank. Combined with a capacity of 5343cc (90mm x 70mm) these features permitted excellent power and torque outputs from 500 to 4500rpm, the actual peak figures being 272bhp (DIN) at 5800rpm and 304lb ft (DIN) of torque at 3600rpm. In other words, because its ultimate destination was a luxury saloon (there was never any question of competition use) the unit had to be as flexible as possible. The alloy crankcase and cylinder block were 116lb lighter than a cast-iron unit would have been and in fact the V12 was just 80lb heavier than the 4.2 litre XK lump. It was also a stiff structure, thanks to a four inch deep skirt below the crank's centreline and iron caps for the seven main bearings, and there was no noticeable noise increase compared with the alternative iron block either. Cast-iron push fit cylinder liners were used and the oil pump was a crescent type, similar to the kind found in an automatic gearbox, mounted on the nose of the crankshaft. The lubrication system also boasted an oil cooler, the water cooled casting being bolted to the step of the sump at the front of the engine. Fifty per cent of the engine oil passed through the cooler during hard driving and because the heat exchanger got its water from the radiator the oil passing through it from a cold start helped warm the engine's coolant up too. The water pump was a conventional vane type, fitted in a housing cast into the front face of the timing cover and driven by a vee belt from the crankshaft pulley.

Although Jaguar had at first envisaged using a new electronic fuel injection system which Brico had under development, in the end a four carburettor layout had to be used when Brico decided not to go into production with the new installation. Each set of three cylinders was fed by a calibrated and sealed Zenith-Stromberg 175CDSE carb, mounted

A beautifully detailed cutaway of the all-aluminium V12 engine. The unit had flat rather than hemispherical cylinder heads and single overhead camshafts for each bank, driven by chains. Four Zenith Stromberg carbs were mounted outside the vee, feeding long induction tracts.

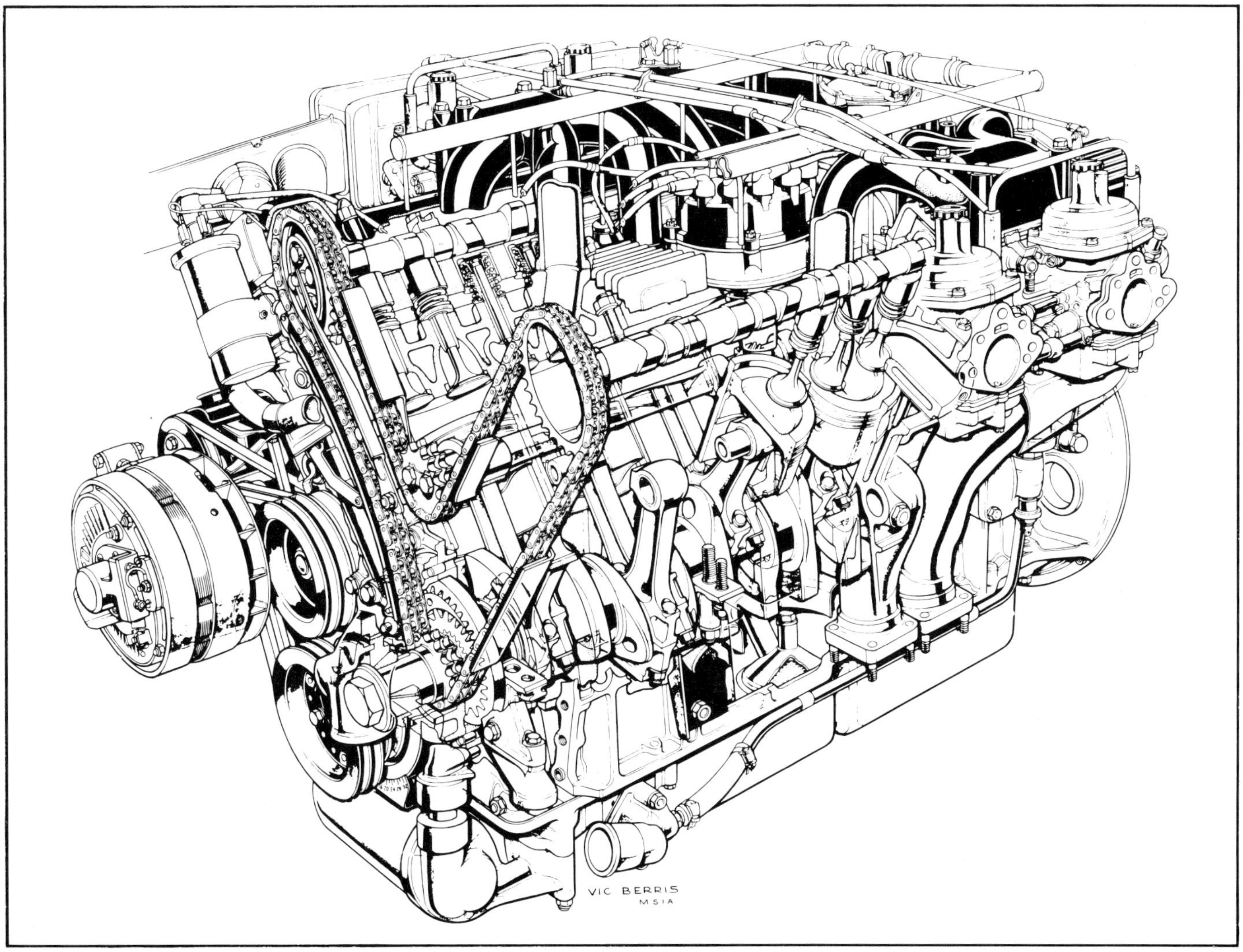

outside the vee of the engine to enable long inlet tracts to be used, giving good ram effects and thus improving mid-range torque. To help the engine cope with emission requirements and to allow it to run on 97 octane fuel a 9 to 1 compression ratio was used.

The camshafts operated the valves directly via bucket tappets working against double valve springs. Chain drive for the cams was retained mainly to keep the length of the engine down (most new engines were going over to belt drive), the 5½ft-long Duplex item being turned by a 21-tooth crankshaft sprocket. An 11in-long blade Morse tensioner was fitted and the back of the chain turned a jackshaft mounted in the vee angle of the engine, its only function in life being to drive the distributor in its position in the centre of the vee.

Because a conventional ignition system with contact breakers needed very skilled attention on a multi-cylinder engine like the V12 (and couldn't meet emission requirements either) Jaguar decided to use the new Lucas OPUS MkII transistorized ignition system, which hadn't yet been seen on a production unit. With this layout the only moving parts were the rotor arm and attendant advance and retard mechanism, the contact breakers being replaced by an electro-magnetic pick-up and amplifier among other things. At first there were some doubts about the reliability of this system, as some early Series 3s suffered from misfires at high rpm that were often put down to a fault on the OPUS unit. The pick-up module, amplifier and the sometimes porous rotor arm were thus modified quite early on and these changes seemed to cure the fault, although a lot of the trouble was quite possibly caused by the type of plug used initially, as Jaguar changed the Champion N9Ys for N10Ys in October 1972. Things were further improved in February 1974 when a high load coil and amplifier were introduced.

From October 1974 onwards all markets, including Britain, got the emission specification engine in their Series 3 V12 E-types, the air pump driven off the water pump pulley pushing air into the exhaust gases just below the exhaust valves to help more complete burning of the waste gases. This resulted in a considerably lower 250bhp at 6000rpm and 288lb ft of torque at 3500rpm, although US market 1974 cars were even worse off thanks to a lower 7.8:1 compression ratio which allowed just 241bhp and 285lb ft of torque.

Originally Jaguar also listed an XK engined version of the Series 3 E-type, alas in full emission specification guise with the twin Stromberg carbs and cross-over preheating system fitted to the last of the US market Series 2s and all XJ6 4.2 saloons. In the end, because of the high demand for the V12, Jaguar decided not to go ahead with

The V12 installed in the Series 3. Fitting the unit into the E-type was fairly straightforward, the main changes being a widened and beefed up subframe and a stonger bulkhead. Accessibility to most major service items was good enough. On its own the V12 only weighed in at 680lb, not that much heavier than the XK unit.

The later twin - rather than four-outlet tailpipe. The four-outlet type tended to rot quickly.

production of this variant, which with only 171bhp would only have been capable of perhaps 125mph. It's interesting to note that four examples of the 4.2 Series 3 did escape from Browns Lane, although at the time of writing only one resides in the UK.

Other changes to the car were fairly extensive, although the basic mixture remained very much as before. The most evident change was that both open and closed models used the 2-plus-2's 8ft 9in wheelbase chassis, which meant that the roadster gained more luggage space behind the seats and increased seat adjustment. Furthermore, the whole floor of the Series 3 cars was lowered to the same levels as the footwells on the previous model, so that even the tallest drivers could now feel comfortable in a two-seater E-type for the first time. To take the greater weight and torsional requirements of the V12 engine the front subframe was strengthened with gusset plates bridging the corners of the upper forward tubes, and there was a tubular tie bar under the engine. The top of the square front crossmember was now detachable to enable the engine to be removed, and some modifications to the tubes and tie brackets gave more wheel clearance for a tighter 36ft turning circle. This modification also had the effect of widening the front track from 50 to 54.6in. The front suspension also gained XJ6 anti-dive geometry, so that, in theory, you could not scrape the lower nose under hard braking on rough ground. This was achieved by inclining the pivot line of the upper wishbones. Another new feature of the front suspension was sealed-for-life upper wishbone mounting bearings, and snail cam adjusters on the torsion bars replacing the vernier method.

By using longer wishbones (from the Mark X/420G) and driveshafts the rear track was increased from 50 to 53in, and wider 6in chromed pressed steel bolt-on wheels came as standard. If these rather boring looking appendages were not to your taste you could always opt for the traditional chrome wire wheels, although whatever your choice Dunlop SP Sport E70 VR15 tyres were fitted. Ventilated Girling front discs were deemed essential for the heavier Series 3, 11.18in in diameter and 0.94in thick, with distance pieces in the otherwise standard calipers to make up for the extra thickness. The inboard rear discs had anti-squeal rings and underbody air ducting to help keep them cool. Like it or not, Adwest power steering was standard on the V12, although to be fair the car would have been near impossible to steer without it. The pump was driven by a vee belt from the crankshaft pulley and the rack was mounted on new L shaped rubber mountings in shear that reduced steering kick-back. The steering column was collapsible and energy absorbing, and was made in two parts joined by a universal joint, with a second UJ joining it to the rack. The same four-speed manual gearbox as used on the six-cylinder cars was the standard fitment on the V12, but with a bigger 10.5in diameter clutch. The automatic option was now available on the open car as well, the latest Borg-Warner Model 12 unit

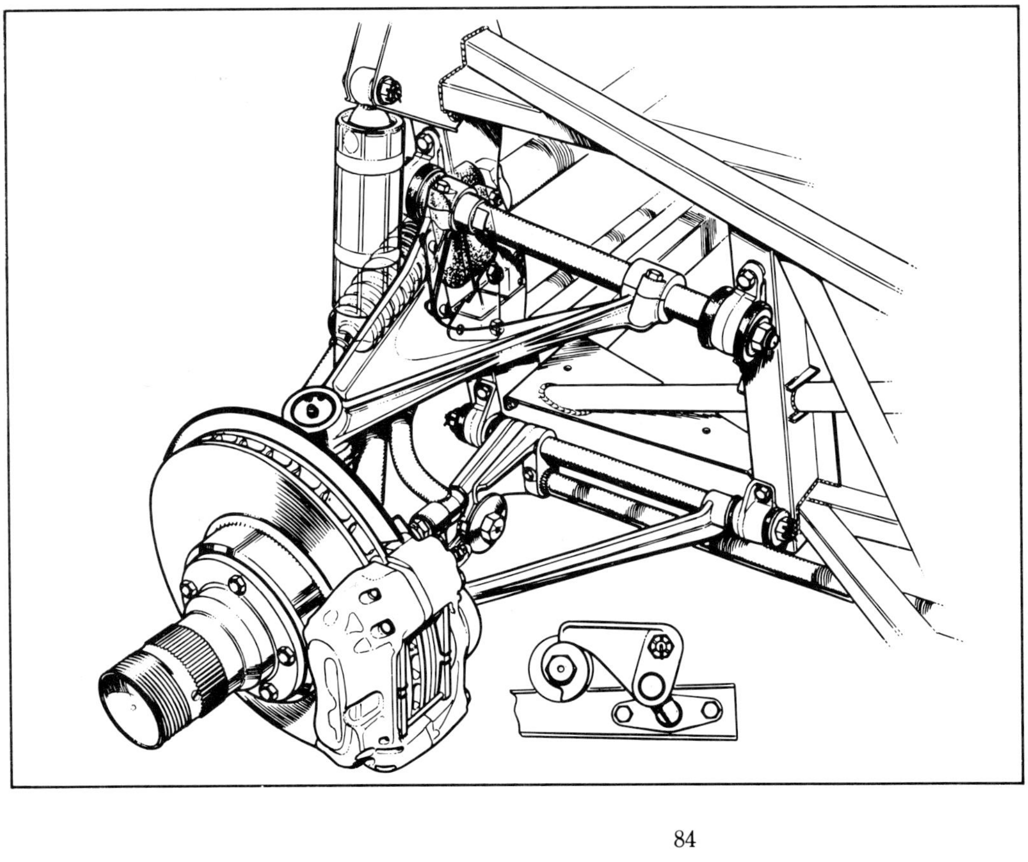

above

Though the whole chassis of the E-type was generally stiffened, the basic layout remained very much as before, as this Autocar *cutaway shows to good effect.*

left

Front suspension detail of the Series 3, showing the angled XJ6-type wishbone mountings (to cancel out nosedive under braking), the new cam method of torsion bar adjustment and the ventilated front disc brakes.

being fitted, with part throttle kickdown operated by manifold depression and positive selection of first and second gear. There was no D2 second-gear start-off facility as on the old Model 8.

Home market cars had a 3.31:1 final drive ratio in manual form and 3.07:1 with the automatic, while cars going to North America used 3.54 and 3.31 ratios. From April 1972 the 3.07:1 ratio was available on manual cars and by March of the following year this was the standard ratio in all markets except North America and Canada, where the 3.31 axle was fitted to all manual cars. A limited slip device came as standard.

On the outside the Series 3 was easy to identify, the biggest change being the new bigger nose intake and chrome 'birdcage' grille, with an additional air scoop below it for the new through-flow ventilation system. Also new were the flared front and rear wheel arches designed to accommodate the wider track. The roadster had the 2-plus-2's screen rake angle and at the back the lights and number plate were mounted on a satin finished plinth. Bumper overriders were now fitted with rubber inserts and on the coupé there was an extractor grille on the rear luggage door for the through-flow ventilation. Hardtop equipped roadsters also had these grilles, on the rear pillars.

Inside, Jaguar had made an attempt at dragging the E-type into the seventies, albeit a rather half-hearted attempt. The facia was still the same old confused but attractive mixture of round white-on-black dials and rocker switches but there was a new, smaller 15in Springall steering wheel with a leather covered rim and satin finished alloy spokes. The seats were covered in perforated leather on their wearing surfaces, with Ambla elsewhere, and those in the front on coupé models were raised to give better forward visibility and more foot room for the rear passengers. They also had a full width operating bar, and the seat reclining levers were extended so the rear seat passengers could pull them when they wanted to get out. Head rests were standard in North America but optional in the UK. In March 1972 a fresh air ventilation system was incorporated, air passing up into rectangular channels in the bonnet and then into ducts alongside the footwells, exhausting through a mushroom nozzle. A push-pull knob controlling a butterfly valve regulated the flow.

The end of production

Despite the lukewarm reception it received from many quarters the V12 E sold reasonably well, and it's interesting to note that during 1974 production actually increased by 35%. However, people were no longer clamouring to buy an E-type in the early seventies and for the first time Jaguar were having to 'push' the car with advertising. Dealers were well stocked up with cars and you could now order an E without having to join a long waiting list, an unheard of situation just a few years before. In any event, by 1974 the writing was on the wall for Jaguar's sports car; it didn't stand much chance of meeting future Federal crash regulations and as usual Jaguar relied very heavily on the American market for sales, 49,032 out of 72,507 E-types produced in total going to the USA. Production of the coupé officially stopped in September 1974 and the roadster stayed on the price list until February of the following year.

As a rather cynical marketing ploy Jaguar painted all but one of the last 50 roadsters (starting at chassis number IS2823) black, and fitted them with chrome wire wheels and a dashboard plaque signed by Sir William Lyons and stating the chassis number. These cars didn't sell as quickly as Jaguar had hoped (most

left

Because the V12 roadster used the 2-plus-2 wheelbase you could now get an automatic gearbox in your open E-type for the first time, the 5.3 car using a Borg-Warner Model 12 unit with three speeds.

far right

The roadster benefited from the wheelbase change as its cabin was now rather roomier, with more available seat adjustment and more space in the footwells. Perforated leather was used on the seat cushions, with Ambla elsewhere. Head restraints were optional in the UK but standard in some other markets.

right

The facia of the Series 3 car was much like that of the Series 2, except for the smaller 15in leather-rimmed Springall steering wheel.

far right

The extra space behind the roadster's seats was used to provide a small luggage platform and a safe box, which was not lockable.

right

Boot of the roadster was always rather shallow. Spare wheel and tool roll are still under the boot floor.

went abroad in the end) and many were sold at quite a bit less than list price, often just £3500. Today one of these cars will set you back a lot more than the most expensive model in the latest Jaguar range . . . The last but one car was painted British Racing green and stayed in this country, while Jaguar kept the last car (Chassis number IS2872) for display and publicity purposes. Though the XJS was supposed to take over from the E-type in 1975 it was actually no replacement, being far too much of a two-door luxury saloon in character and a million miles away from the raw appeal of the E. Since then it has looked as though Browns Lane would never build a true replacement for the E-type but as this is being written news has emerged of an 'F-type' successor to be built in the early 1990s.

All but one of the last fifty E-types were painted black and had a plaque like this mounted on the glove box lid, signed by William Lyons and giving the chassis number. The last but one car was painted British racing green to special order.

The last E-type was built in February 1975 and is pictured here with the workers who were responsible for it. Production of the coupé had ended some months earlier in 1974.

A V12 roadster alongside the car that followed it, the XJS, in this case the much later cabriolet. An ugly car to many eyes, the XJS was more 'touring' than sporting and not a true E-type replacement.

What to look for in the Series 3

The V12 engine is so strong and understressed that it probably presents fewer snags for the buyer than an XK engine does. However, being all aluminium in construction, it is less tolerant of inadequate maintenance. Most of the things that do go wrong with the engine cannot really be tackled by a home mechanic due to the unit's size and complexity, though having said that the V12 is probably not quite as complicated as it looks when you first lift the bonnet.

You should turn your attention first to the cooling system, because it is essential that this engine is kept adequately cool and never allowed to overheat. This can cause the cylinder head to distort and virtually 'weld' itself to the block, and getting the two to part is a good day's struggle for a specialist. Check that the coolant is not low and ask the owner if the engine tends to use water, as either of these conditions can cause head gasket failure which in turn leads to overheating. The water should look as though it has some anti-freeze in it.

Oil leaks are another problem with this unit. Many are only minor drips from the oil filter housing or from small pipes that have perished with age, all of these being easy to put right. Beware though of an oil leak from the bell-housing area, which indicates that the rear main bearing oil seal has gone, and that's a very costly engine and crankshaft out job to put right. Try shaking the water pump pulley to see if there is any play in the bearing, and with the engine running listen for rattles at the front end of the unit indicating a worn jackshaft assembly. Bearing trouble is hard to pinpoint but try listening with your ear as close as possible to the sump. The oil pressure can still be the correct 60-80psi at 3500rpm with the engine hot even when one of the main bearings has gone. Look for a cracked exhaust manifold as these are extremely awkward to get at – you have to remove the carbs and inlet manifolds to remove them. Timing chain noise is possible and, although the V12 does not burn oil in the way the XK does, you may get blue smoke from the exhaust when the throttle is blipped after it's been ticking over for a while, which means bore wear.

Though most of them have been sorted out you may still get the odd early car that has a Lucas OPUS electronic ignition system that likes to play up a little. The wiring is often as much of a problem as the unit itself, the wires that go across the centre of the engine tending to crack up in places when they get too hot, causing tracking of the circuits out into the engine. A faulty switching action in the amplifier causes the car not to start, and the only thing that can cure this effectively is a new amplifier. In the distributor the 12 ferrite rods in the timing disc tend to fall out, causing the engine to 'miss', and this is a difficult one to sort out unless you look at the disc itself. Brand new timing discs sometimes have one or two ferrite rods missing, too.

left

The last E-type nears the end of the production line in 1975.

Looking at the rest of the car it's worth remembering that the four-speed gearbox is under more stress in the Series 3 due to the V12 engine's torque, so first and reverse gear are prone to break. Clutch judder is also a problem with the Series 3, but other than this the V12 problems are basically those of the six cylinder car. There are few spares problems, if any, though interchangeability of parts between other E-types is if anything a little more limited. The Series 1 XJ12 and Daimler Double Six saloons used the same engine and automatic gearbox, and if you are not interested in originality then you could fit the fuel-injected unit used later, or even the more powerful 'fireball' head engine used in the current V12 XJS and XJ12 Series 3.

Restoration

Anything is possible but on the whole the V12 engine is not one that can be taken on by the home mechanic. It's not that it's especially complicated – in fact having just one camshaft per bank it is less complex than the XK in some ways – it's just that there is so much of it, plus a maze of fairly high tech ancillaries. In any event the unit hardly ever goes wrong in a big way and most of the problems are with the bits that hang on the engine such as the electronic ignition.

The bodywork goes just as rotten and is just as hard to repair as on the six-cylinder cars but with V12 values now going up so quickly you at least have a good chance of recouping your restoration cost when you come to sell the car, especially if it happens to be a roadster.

Running and maintenance

Running a V12 E-type will not be a cheap business by any means, especially in terms of fuel consumption. A hard driven manual car will return only 13mpg and even the light footed will hardly ever get more than about 16 miles to the gallon. Automatic cars are even worse, of course, and on a fast run the 18 gallon fuel tank has a range of only 200 miles, which is why V12 owners always take their credit cards with them when they go out for a blast!

However, as a car for everyday or at least regular usage the V12 is a better bet than the six-cylinder car in many respects, having more room than the old roadster so that the long legged can feel comfortable in the car, along with a quieter engine and better road holding if not handling. The coupé version is a very relaxed motorway mile-eater and with the best part of 300bhp on tap both versions have really stunning performance.

The engine is a daunting sight when you first open the bonnet but once you know your way around it is reasonably straightforward to maintain and much of the work is carried out on the same principles as on the XK unit. There is just much more of everything and accessibility is not all that good – very often you have to remove five items just to service one component. Having said that, most of the service items that require attention every 3000 miles are easy enough to get at and few people would have any trouble changing the plugs (they are in the centre of the vee), oil and oil filter. The alternator is in an awkward position (and oil tends to drip onto it from various places), and it's as well to change the plug leads fairly regularly as they are very long and get hot, causing a lot of rough running problems.

The tappets are adjusted in just the same way as on the XK engine although the task is made easier if anything because the V12 has only a single overhead camshaft for each bank. On the cooling system the front of the head silts up, and because of this it's as well to flush the unit through every now and again. As already mentioned the V12 engine should never be allowed to run low on water, and as with all aluminium engines anti-freeze should be kept in the cooling system all year round if internal corrosion is to be avoided.

Cost guidelines

During the darkest days of the seventies fuel crisis you would have had trouble giving a petrol-guzzling V12 E-type away, but just lately these cars, particularly in roadster form, have become very fashionable. They tend now to be the most valuable of the E-type range, and things look set to stay that way. Only the 3.8 roadster can begin to rival the V12 roadster's value, though a fully restored Series 3 in virtually concours order can bring as much as £10,000 more than an equally good early car. By way of comparison you could buy a truly superb closed 4.2 car for the price of a superficially tidy (but probably rotten) open V12. Why this should be so is hard to pinpoint, but it must have something to do with the 5.3's comfortable, easygoing character, which makes the car appealing to rich enthusiasts

For all its faults one thing the Series 3 did have in abundance was performance. Here an Autocar *road test car leaps off the line to record a 0-60 time of 6.4secs and 0-100 in 15.4!*

who want a classic that's a little more comfortable, if rather less sporting, than the six-cylinder models. Rough Series 3 roadsters are now being snapped up at quite high prices as soon as they come onto the market because speculators know what the car will bring when fully restored. One of the commemorative 5.3 roadsters could virtually command its own price, though these are rarely seen for sale.

There's a substantial difference in price between roadsters and coupés, a closed car may only fetch between a third and half of the price of an open car and may not cost much more than a standard wheelbase six-cylinder fixed-head. I am told, however, that V12 coupés will go up in value considerably before too long. Automatics are available in both body styles but because of the 'soft' character of the V12 they don't affect values so much, and I suspect many coupé buyers may actually prefer the auto. Wire wheels are obviously desirable.

In a nutshell

The Series 3 E-type is a very different animal in character from its predecessors and tends to attract a very different type of owner. If anything it beats the pure-bred Series 1 in the popularity stakes at the moment. The cars have a lot going for them, after all; few cars this side of a Ferrari have more vivid performance, they are comfortable in comparison with the six-cylinder cars and the engine tends to be even more reliable because it is so understressed. In other words, these are easygoing and easy-to-live-with E-types, representing far less trouble for the man who isn't too interested in the ultimate in sporty handling but cares a great deal about his image down at the pub on a Sunday morning. On the down side, they generally cost more to buy than a Series 1 or 2, are more costly to run and there is little a DIY man can do if anything major goes wrong with the engine.

SPECIFICATIONS

E-type 5.3 Series 3 roadster and 2-plus-2

Engine	60° V12
Construction	All alloy
Main bearings	Seven
Bore/Stroke	90mm×70mm
Capacity	5343cc
Valves	Single OHC per bank
Compression ratio	9:1
Fuel system	4 Zenith 175CDSE carburettors
Power	272bhp (net) at 5850rpm 250bhp (net) at 6000rpm (emission engine)
Torque	304lb ft at 3600rpm 288lb ft at 3500rpm (emission engine)
Transmission	Four-speed manual or Borg-Warner Model 12 three-speed automatic
Top gear	24.7mph per 1000rpm (manual) 26.4mph per 1000rpm (automatic)
Final drive	3.07:1 (optional 2.93, 3.27, 3.31, 3.54, 3.77, 4.09)
Brakes	Girling discs all round, 11.2in (vented) front, 10.4in rear
Suspension, front	Ind. by anti-dive wishbones and torsion bars, with Girling telescopic dampers
Suspension, rear	Ind. by lower wishbones with radius arms and twin coil springs, with Girling telescopic dampers. Upper location by halfshafts
Steering	Rack and pinion, standard power assistance
Wheels/tyres	Bolt-on pressed steel or optional centre-lock wire wheels, 6in rims. E70 VR 15in tyres
Body	All-steel body, monocoque up to front bulkhead with space subframe at front. 2-door roadster or 2-plus-2 3-door coupé

DIMENSIONS

Length	15ft 6in
Width	5ft 6¼in
Height	4ft 1in (roadster) 4ft 3in (coupé)
Wheelbase	8ft 9in
Unladen weight	28¾cwt (roadster) 29½cwt (coupé)

Production History

3.8

MARCH 1961	Jaguar E-type 3.8 roadster and fixed-head coupé introduced at Geneva Motor Show. All new monocoque body with space subframe at front, two seats, and rear luggage door on FHC. 265bhp (gross) three-carb version of 3781cc XK engine with four-speed Moss gearbox. Four-wheel Dunlop disc brakes and all independent suspension. Prices (including purchase tax) £2097 for roadster and £2196 for fixed-head coupé.
JUNE 1961	Larger oil pump introduced.
AUGUST 1961	Water deflector now fitted on front stub axle carrier.
SEPTEMBER 1961	Internal bonnet locks introduced.
OCTOBER 1961	Revisions include cast-iron rather than alloy crankshaft pulley, automatic fanbelt tensioner, new C42 dynamo with RB340 regulator and new fuel pump and tank with improved filter and one-piece drain plug. Larger rear hub bearings and propshaft universal joints, longer rear road springs.
DECEMBER 1961	New asbestos rope type crankshaft rear oil seal, brass bush in brake and clutch pedal housing replaced by self-lubricating impregnated plastic bush.
JANUARY 1961	Revised throttle arrangement, air balance pipe redesigned, modified brake master cylinders and new Mintex M33 pad material. Seat belt attachment points now provided.
FEBRUARY 1962	Big end clearances reduced, method of retaining bonnet hinges to front subframe revised (bolt retaining hinges to cross tube), and heel wells introduced.
MARCH 1962	Revised cylinder head gasket with bigger head stud holes, and combined ignition switch/steering lock fitted to all German market cars.
APRIL 1962	Electrically heated rear screen now optional.
MAY 1962	Drilled inlet camshaft to reduce cold starting noise, brake power lever and pedals altered to increase mechanical advantage, throttle pedal on RHD cars modified to help heel and toe operation, 'sealed for life' universal joints now fitted to propshaft. FHC body now has modified outer rear wings, bootlid gutter, bootlid shell, hinge for bootlid, tail panel, lid for petrol filler, door shell, door light. Roadster doors also modified, detachable hardtop now available.

JUNE 1962	Modified sump filter gasket, Duplex water pump belt with revised pulleys. New oil seal container and felt oil seal fitted to outer fulcrum shaft. Modified rear bulkhead to allow extra rearward seat travel, new cantilever-type jack.
JULY 1962	Modified clutch master cylinder/fluid reservoir, solid forged rear axle halfshafts to replace tubular shafts, modified handbrake cable, compensator and calipers.
SEPTEMBER 1962	Longer inlet valves and guides, modified pistons, rings and connecting rods with additional big end lug drillings. Revised fixings for rear brake calipers. Internal fuel pipe material changed from Vulkolan to nylon.
OCTOBER 1962	Larger main bearing dowels introduced, pattern change on embossed aluminium finishers on instrument panel, front finisher panel and gearbox cover. US and Canadian market cars now 3.3:1 axle ratio as standard, home market and other countries now 3.07:1. 2.93:1 option discontinued.
NOVEMBER 1962	'Sealed for life' rear axle halfshaft joints and quicklift thermostat now fitted.
DECEMBER 1962	Modified bootlid prop on FHC.
JANUARY 1963	Rear gearbox mounting revised.
MARCH 1963	Radiator header tank revised with higher pressure cap.
JUNE 1963	Thicker (½ inch) rear brake discs, new calipers, modified caliper mountings and final drive casing. Delrin needle valve fitted to carburettors with new float chamber lid and hinged lever. 22D6 distributor replaces DMBZ6 type. Modified oil pump.
AUGUST 1963	Handbrake compensator inner lever link replaced by inner fork end and outer fork end, allowing greater adjustment.
SEPTEMBER 1963	Exhaust valves made of improved material, 3.54:1 rear axle ratio standard on American and Canadian market cars.
OCTOBER 1963	Improved quarterlight catches on FHC.
NOVEMBER 1963	New rear axle breather unit.
JANUARY 1964	Halfshaft universal joint shrouds and brake fluid reservoir cap cover now fitted. Also modification to allow opening of roadster boot, if cable breaks, via hole in number plate panel.
MARCH 1964	Modified pistons with chamfer and oil drain holes below control ring to improve oil consumption. Laycock diaphragm clutch introduced.
MAY 1964	Intermediate lower timing chain damper secured to bosses in block rather than to timing chain bracket.
JUNE 1964	Modified distributor fitted to 9:1 cr engines.

4.2 Series 1

OCTOBER 1964	E-type 4.2 roadster and fixed-head coupé introduced. Bigger 4236cc engine with more torque, same power. Also alternator replaces dynamo, negative earth electrical system, twin electric fuel pumps, pre-engaged starter, new Lockheed vacuum booster. Most important change is new all-synchromesh Jaguar-designed four-speed gearbox. Revised interior with new seats, glove box on transmission tunnel, black finished instrument panel. Prices (including purchase tax) £1896 for roadster and £1992 for fixed-head coupé.
NOVEMBER 1964	Chamfered idler gear to reduce gearbox noise, finisher panel on transmission tunnel revised, chrome bezel at top of panel for gearlever gauntlet and chrome ferrule at top of gauntlet discontinued.
JANUARY 1965	Pocket under rear side windows deleted, plastic rather than moquette trim on FHC rear wheel arches.
FEBRUARY 1962	Front disc brake shields fitted.
MARCH 1965	Modified roller bearing fitted to gearbox constant pinion shaft.
APRIL 1965	Standard axle ratio now 3.07:1, except USA and Canada.
DECEMBER 1965	Hazard warning light now fitted as standard.
FEBRUARY 1966	Constant pinion shaft changed to include oil thrower. FHC window frame seals changed from felt to flocked runner.
MARCH 1966	2-plus-2 E-type introduced, 9in longer than standard FHC with revised rear bulkhead to accommodate the rear seat with its foldable rear squab. Interior now features variable-direction air outlet nozzles. Borg-Warner Model 8 automatic transmission available for extra £140. Improvements for all models include seven-tooth pinion to improve steering with radial tyres, new brake and clutch master cylinders and pedal housings.
APRIL 1966	Switch incorporated in heated rear screen circuit.
MAY 1966	Shield fitted to alternator.
SEPTEMBER 1966	Modified carb assembly with low lift cam to reduce engine speed with choke operated.
NOVEMBER 1966	Retaining washer fitted to further secure gear lever; clutch/brake master cylinders modified to improve pedal angles, throttle pedal angle also revised.
JANUARY 1967	Valve guides fitted with circlips to give positive location in cylinder head.
MARCH 1967	Oil seals fitted to inlet valve guides.
MAY 1967	New road wheels introduced with straight spokes and forged centre hubs.
JULY 1967	Headlight covers discontinued.

SEPTEMBER 1967 PowrLok diff no longer standard, except in Canada and USA.

JANUARY 1968 US Federal specification introduced, grease nipples reintroduced on halfshaft universal joints.

FEBRUARY 1968 Replaceable fuel line filter introduced.

APRIL 1968 Solid-skirt Hepworth and Grandage pistons fitted instead of Brico split skirt, revised water pump pulley and belt to increase pump speed and flow rate. Also federal spec. door casings and linings fitted to RHD cars.

JULY 1968 Water temperature gauge with zonal markings only replaces calibrated gauge.

4.2 Series 2

OCTOBER 1968 Series 2 E-type introduced. Outward changes include bigger, raised bumpers with larger sidelight/flasher units underneath, larger air intake, bigger headlamp units, new rectangular rear lights and repositioned reversing lights under bumper. Also crossflow radiator with twin electric fans. Extensive emission equipment on Federal spec. models, bigger Girling-made brakes, collapsible steering column, optional Adwest power steering and stronger chrome plated wire wheels. Screen rake angle of 2-plus-2 increased from 46½ to 53½ degrees and many cabin changes including new seats, recessed door handles, rocker switches rather than toggle switches. Prices: roadster £2163, FHC £2273, 2-plus-2 £2668

DECEMBER 1968 Steering column lock now fitted.

JANUARY 1969 Lucas 11AC alternator with side entry cable introduced and non-eared hub caps now standard on RHD cars.

MARCH 1969 Better clutch with higher rated diaphragm spring, reducing tendency to slip. Petrol tank upper panel redesigned.

APRIL 1969 Load-shedding starter/ignition switch introduced.

MAY 1969 Camshaft covers now secured by countersunk screw at front centre position. Perforated leather trim and modified head restraints introduced.

JUNE 1969 Cylinder block drain tap replaced by plug.

AUGUST 1969 Engine number stamping relocated on crankcase bellhousing flange on L/H side of engine. Provision for head restraints in seats.

OCTOBER 1969 Mercury cell clock replaced by battery operated instrument, demister tube extension fitted to 2-plus-2.

NOVEMBER 1969 New camshafts with redesigned profiles to give quieter valve operation over wider range of valve clearances and allow longer periods between adjustment.

JANUARY 1970	Camshaft covers drilled for warm air duct, ballast resistor ignition fitted, key alarm facility ignition switch on USA and Canada cars.
MARCH 1970	Revised clutch operating rod to accommodate wider setting tolerances.
MAY 1970	New handbrake lever assembly with increased length and end portion angled upwards on 2-plus-2.
AUGUST 1970	Larger diameter torsion bars and new crankshaft distance piece with 'O' ring.
OCTOBER 1970	Revised exhaust camshaft without oilway drilling in back of cams to reduce oil consumption, modified thermostat.

5.3 Series 3

MARCH 1971	E-type 5.3 Series 3 roadster and fixed-head coupé introduced. New alloy 272bhp 5343cc V12 in much revised bodyshell. Both open and closed models now have 2-plus-2 wheelbase with flared wheel arches, bigger air intake with grille, wider pressed steel wheels (wires optional). Front disc brakes ventilated, front and rear tracks increased slightly, power steering now standard. Four-speed manual gearbox or Borg-Warner Model 12 automatic. Heating and ventilation system improved, new steering wheel. Prices: Roadster £3122, 2-plus-2 £3369, automatic £160 extra.
JULY 1971	RHD automatic cars get modified brake pedal components to improve left foot clearance, red marking deleted from water temperature gauge.
NOVEMBER 1971	Connector inserted in windscreen washer bottle tubing to simplify removal of bonnet.
DECEMBER 1971	Modified crankshaft thrust washer fitted and handbrake assembly made common to LHD and RHD cars.
MARCH 1972	Improved heater and choke controls.
APRIL 1972	3.07:1 rear axle ratio now optional on manual cars. Fresh air vents fitted with control levers in cockpit, Waso steering lock replaces Britax, securing brackets fitted to centre cross beam and lower rear damper mounting for shipping. Remote control door mirror fitted to USA and Canada cars.
MAY 1972	Revised starter motor and flywheel/driven plate, lighter piston assembly. Seat belt alarm system fitted to USA cars, rear seats fixed.
JUNE 1972	Revised adjuster cam with larger cam profile on torsion bar, forward section of engine rainshield now secured to an additional support mounted on front inlet manifold. Oil feed hole deleted on shell bearings to connecting rod big ends.
AUGUST 1972	Printed circuit ballast resistor introduced.

OCTOBER 1972	Deletion of small end oil feed drilling in connecting rods, modified water pump and simplified water hose system. N10Y plugs specified instead of N9Y.
DECEMBER 1972	Modified pinion valve assembly on rack and pinion due to isolated instance of self steer. Revised main bearings with improved lining material. Sealed fuel system with carbon canister.
JANUARY 1973	New needle roller bearing in gearbox, revised power rack and pinion assembly.
FEBRUARY 1973	Thermostatic vacuum switch fitted to RH rear coolant branch pipe, and associated hoses deleted from all non-exhaust emission engines. New air injection pump with integral air filter fitted to all exhaust emission engines. Coil and ballast resistor moved to RH rear of engine for improved access to engine drive belts. Improved XJ12-type Borg-Warner Model 12 automatic gearbox now fitted.
MARCH 1973	Axle ratio on all USA/Canada cars now 3.3:1 (3.54:1 no longer fitted to manual cars). 3.07:1 fitted for all other markets. New petrol filter assembly with metal filter bowl, dispensing with fuel stop tap. Filter relocated to extreme right of luggage boot bulkhead panel. Two-outlet exhaust pipe with modified silencer replacing four-outlet fantail pipe. Engines to ECE 15 European emissions spec. for Germany only.
APRIL 1973	Revised air ducts to rear brakes with increased ground clearance, now fitted during assembly and no longer supplied for dealer to fit.
MAY 1973	XJ12 crankshaft damper fitted to standardize.
JUNE 1973	Phosphor bronze rear hub spacer (to eliminate click in rear suspension) added.
JULY 1973	Improved oil pump assembly with new housing.
OCTOBER 1973	Cars for USA/Canada fitted with revised camshaft with different profile. Modified synchromesh operating sleeve to prevent jumping out of foward gears. New gearbox countershaft of revised material.
FEBRUARY 1974	High load coil and amplifier introduced to improve plug performance.
SEPTEMBER 1974	Fixed-head coupé discontinued.
OCTOBER 1974	All markets except Canada, USA and Japan get ECE European emission spec. engines.
NOVEMBER 1973	Revised valve tappets.
FEBRUARY 1975	Roadster discontinued.

Series 3 coupé, with optional wire wheels, owned by Frank Taylor.

Until March 1973 the V12 E-type had this exotic looking four-pipe 'fantail' exhaust, which tended to rot quickly. The grille on the rear door was for the through-flow ventilation.

The Series 3 coupé, only available as a 2-plus-2. This model was discontinued some months before the roadster and is thus slightly rarer.

Interior of the Series 3 coupé.

The all-alloy 5.3-litre V12 engine fitted in the Series 3 – not as nice to look at as the XK, maybe, and much more thirsty, but smoother and more powerful.

PRODUCTION FIGURES

	RHD	LHD	TOTAL
3.8 Roadster	942	6885	7827
3.8 Fixed-Head Coupé	1798	5871	7669
4.2 Roadster	1182	8366	9548
4.2 Fixed-Head Coupé	1957	5813	7770
4.2 2-plus-2	1378	4220	5598
4.2 S2 Roadster	775	7852	8627
4.2 S2 2-plus-2	1040	4286	5326
5.3 S3 Roadster	1871	6119	7990
5.3 S3 2-plus-2	2115	5182	7297

Total Production	
3.8	15,496
4.2	22,916
4.2 S2	18,808
5.3 S3	15,287
TOTAL	72,507

Jaguar Clubs

The E-type has always been popular on the track in club events. Malcolm Hamilton of Stockport Motor Services currently runs one of the most successful cars in Modsports events. This 3.8 coupé is pictured at Oulton Park.

Jaguar Drivers' Club

When Raymond Playford put forward the idea of a Jaguar club in 1956 he initially met with very strong opposition from Sir William Lyons, who some 18 years previously, in 1938, had been embarrassed by the old SS Car Club when its treasurer absconded with the club funds! He only agreed to the formation of the JDC when it was decided that the directors would be nominated by Jaguar Cars. Eventually, in May 1956, the club's inaugural meeting was held, and formal recognition from Browns Lane and the RAC was given six months later. Sir William Lyons resisted all further attempts at forming a rival club and up until recently the Drivers' Club has been the only officially recognized body for Jaguar enthusiasts. Since 1956 the JDC has grown rapidly, with separate registers for all models from the early Swallows to the latest XJ. The Club has a very full competition programme, with plenty of opportunities for owners with suitably equipped cars to take part in all manner of sprints, hillclimbs and race meetings, and of course the social calendar is very active, with meetings and individual register events during the spring and summer months. In 1981 and 1986 the E-type Register even organized trips to Switzerland to commemorate the car's introduction at the Geneva Motor Show in 1961, which says something about the enthusiasm these cars still generate. Currently the Drivers' Club has just over 10,000 members worldwide, spread over 59 regions, and produces an excellent club magazine called *Jaguar Driver*, a very professional 70-odd-page publication with plenty of colour and an individual news section for each register. Sadly, the JDC no longer runs a spares scheme (although certain registers can still supply many items) and the ending of this service planted the first seeds of discontent within the club, causing the formation of the offshoot Jaguar Enthusiasts' Club in 1984. There have been all kinds of upheavals and upsets since then (Jaguar cars no longer officially recognize the JDC only) and as I write the problems continue.

For more details contact Jaguar House, 18 Stuart Street, 18 Stuart Street, Luton, Beds LU1 2SL (tel: 0582 419332).

Jaguar Enthusiasts' Club

To say that the Jaguar Enthusiasts' Club had a turbulent birth would be something of an understatement. Without going into the sordid details, back in 1984 Nigel Thorley, Bob Archard and nine other JDC members (including almost the whole of the MkI and MkII committee) resigned from the JDC because they were dissatisfied with the way the club was moving away from its roots and was, in their view, becoming less interested in the needs of members with older cars, an attitude typified by the discontinuation of the spares operation. Thorley and Co. now believed there was a genuine need for a Jaguar club offering a good spares service and technical advice to its members, and with this in mind they formed the Jaguar Enthusiasts' Club on December 1st 1984. All kinds of accusations began to fly between the two clubs almost immediately, but once the dust had settled it became obvious that the JEC really was offering a viable alternative to the long established Drivers' Club. The Club magazine *Jaguar Enthusiast* was widely acclaimed as an excellent effort by any standards, and the JEC quickly got to work organizing a really useful spares and breakdown service as well as an eight-round 'Classic Cat' challenge race series for pre-'68 standard cars, in conjunction with the BARC.

Since them the Enthusiasts' Club has grown very quickly; at the time of writing it has well over 4000 members. The spares department continues to grow, there's a very useful spares location service and the club has also begun to remanufacture special tools like timing chain adjusters, rear hub puller sets, clutch alignment tools, engine support bars, etc. Restoration seminars, cheaper insurance and free technical advice from experts based in the North and South of England are other benefits.

For further details write to Jaguar Enthusiasts' Club, Freepost, Aldershot, Hants GU12 5BR.

Specialists

Whatever other problems you may have running or restoring your E-type, finding spares or restoration expertise should never present any real snags. You could write down the list of parts that are unobtainable at any one time on the back of a postage stamp, and generally speaking the majority of 'cowboy' Jaguar restoration establishments have disappeared from the scene in the past few years. The Jaguar Specialists' Association can take some of the credit for this, and certainly any firm that displays their symbol has been approved and should provide a good service, though that doesn't mean that many non-JSA members aren't perfectly competent.

The Jaguar Enthusiasts' Club publishes a useful list of Jaguar specialists and services for its members, entries being 'star' graded according to feedback, good or bad, that the club gets from members. Companies which consistently get bad reports are deleted from the list, which is fair enough.

What follows isn't a fully comprehensive survey of every Jaguar specialist in Britain (there just isn't enough room for that) but simply a random list of some of the well known, and sometimes not so well known, firms supplying parts and restoration services for the E-type up and down the country.

General parts suppliers

Martin E. Robey, Pool Road, Camp Hill Industrial Estate, Nuneaton, Warwickshire (tel: 0203 386903)

British Sportscar Centre, 303 Goldhawk Road, London W12 8EZ (tel: 01 748 7824)

Olaf P. Lund & Son, 40 Upper Dean Street, Birmingham B5 4SG (tel: 021 622 1384 or 021 622 5585)

Norman Motors, 100 Mill Lane, London NW6 (tel: 01 431 0940)

SNG Barratt, The Old Workhouse, Union Lane, Trysull, Wolverhampton, West Midlands (tel: 0902 892307)

SC Jaguar Components, 13 Cobham Way, Gatwick Road, Crawley, West Sussex RH10 2RX (tel: 0293 547841-4)

F.B Components, 31-41 Edgeway Road, Marston, Oxford (tel: 0865 724646)

M & C Wilson, 25 Retford Road, Blyth, Nr Worksop (tel: 0909 76693)

Classic Spares, 501-503 Southbury Road, Enfield, Middlesex (tel: 01 805 5534)

Accessory and Motor Supplies, Unit A8, Faraday Road, London Road Industrial Estate, Newbury, Berkshire (tel: 0635 4469)

Minters, Brackwell Farm, Lower Winchendon, Aylesbury, Bucks (tel: 0844 291390)

Maple Corner Spares, Ford Street, Stockport, Cheshire (tel: 061 429 7945)

Trim suppliers and retrimming

Suffolk and Turley, Kelsey Close, Attleborough Fields Industrial Estate, Nuneaton, Warwickshire (tel: 0203 381429)

Barry Hankinson, Claypits House, Much Birch, Hereford (tel: 0989 65789)

Eles Leather-Vinyl Auto Products, Unit 26, Court Road Industrial Estate, Cwmbran, Gwent (tel: 06333 70652 daytime, 06333 75665 evenings)

The Trim Centre, Oaston Road, Whitacre Industrial Estate, Nuneaton, Warwickshire (tel: 0203 374796)

Leather Renovations, Bransgore Garage, Bransgore, Nr Christchurch, Dorset (tel: 0425 74060)

S.P Aldrige, Attwoods Showroom and Workshop, St Marks Road, Chapel Ash, Wolverhampton, W Midlands (tel: 0902 341166)

General restoration specialists

Martin E. Robey, Pool Road, Camp Hill Industrial Estate, Nuneaton, Warwickshire (tel: 0203 386903)

Southern Classics, MWG House, Hanworth Lane, Chertsey, Surrey (tel: 09328 67671)

Eagle Racing, Chartsutton, Nr Maidstone, Kent (tel: 0622 843312)

Kearns-Richards Services, Carrington Road, Stockport (tel: 061 477 1817) (formerly **Stockport Services**)

Advanced Garage Engineering Ltd, 95 Mitcham Lane, Streatham, London (tel: 01 677 1298)

Circuit Motors, 3 Brackley Road, Silverstone, Northants (tel: 0327 857206)

Tower Hill Garage, Crossroads, Chipperfield, Herts (tel: 092 77 64114)

M.R Buckeridge, Airdale Works, Otley Road, Shipley, West Yorkshire (tel: 0274 589389)

G.B Panels, 45 The Drive, Caldecote, Nuneaton, Warwickshire (tel: 0203 341925)

Philips Garage, 206 Bradford Street, Deritend, Birmingham (tel: 021 772 2000)

Jaguar Craft Ltd, 444 Ackroyd Drive, (off Bursett Road), London E3 (tel: 01 980 1190)

Martin Smith, The Old Mill Workshop, Mill Farm Buildings, Lower Winchendon, Nr Aylesbury, Bucks (tel: 0844 290056)

DK Engineering, Unit D, 200 Rickmansworth Road, Watford, Herts (tel: 0923 55246)

DKS Sporting Cars Ltd, 36 Hazlemere Road, Penn, Bucks (tel: 049481 3050)

Engine specialists

Forward Engineering Company Ltd, 780 Kingsbury Road, Erdington, Birmingham (tel: 021 384 6000)

J.S.C, 28 Coventry Street, Coventry, West Midlands (tel: 0203 455602)

Crow Engineering Ltd, 1 Selinas Lane, Dagenham, Essex (tel: 01 592 6272)

A.J Turner, Hockley Industrial Estate, Hooley Lane, Redhill, Surrey (tel: 0737 68114)

LDS, 14-20 Willow Way, Sydenham, Kent (tel: 01 291 1999)

Kearns Richards Service, Stamford Works, Atlantic Street, Broadheath, Altrincham, Cheshire (tel: 061 928 2897)

Acknowledgments

I couldn't have written this book without the help of Malcolm Hamilton of Stockport Motor Services (soon to become Kearns Richards Service). A specialist in and a successful racer of E-types, Malcolm is always very busy yet had time to give me the benefit of his considerable knowledge. Mark Hamilton of Hampson Motor Trust in Winsford, Cheshire, always has a large selection of E-types for sale and very kindly brought the superb 3.8 and V12 roadsters to the photo shoot up in the Derwent Valley on a cold day in February. Thanks also to Frank Taylor and his wife for bringing their lovely V12 coupé and to Malcolm Hamilton again for supplying the green 3.8 fixed-head coupé at such short notice. Many of the black and white restoration photos were taken at Martin E. Robey's, so thanks to Martin for letting us wander round his workshops.

Picture Acknowledgments

The publishers are grateful to the following for supplying the pictures reproduced in this book: *Autocar, Autosport, Classic and Sportscar,* Haymarket Motoring Photo Library, Quadrant Picture Library, Jaguar Cars. Richard G. Bailey, Roger Clinkscales.

CLASSIC
AND SPORTSCAR
HIGH NOON
JAGUAR v FERRARI v ASTON MARTIN

CLASSIC
AND SPORTSCAR
SUMMERTIME
FUN

CLASSIC
AND SPORTSCAR
BRUTE FORCE
BIG HEALEY SUPERPROFILE
FREE INSIDE : BUGATTI SUPPLEMENT

CLASSIC
AND SPORTSCAR
LA DOLCE VITA
RESTORATION SPECIAL
PLUS: 1987 CONCOURS CHAMPION

CLASSIC
AND SPORTSCAR
SO CHEAP
IT'S CRIMINAL

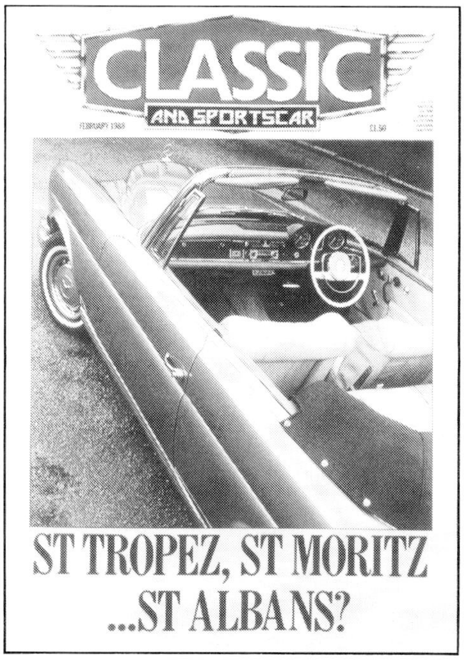
CLASSIC
AND SPORTSCAR
ST TROPEZ, ST MORITZ
…ST ALBANS?